PATRICK GREG

THE LIMBS IN THE LOCH MURDERER

THE SHOCKING TRUE STORY OF BRITAIN'S MOST SAVAGE KILLER

D1079989

JOHN BLAKE

London W14 9PB, England

www.johnblakepublishing.co.uk

First published in paperback in 2011

ISBN: 978 1 84358 284 7

British Library Cataloguing-in-Publication Data:

A catalogue record for this book is available from the British Library.

Design by www.envydesign.co.uk

Printed in Great Britain by CPI Bookmarque, Croydon CR0 4TD

1 3 5 7 9 10 8 6 4 2

Papers used by John Blake Publishing are natural, recyclable products
made from wood grown in sustainable forests. The manufacturing
processes conform to the environmental regulations
of the country of origin.

Contents

Timeline

1987 Beggs convicted for the murder of Barry Oldham, whose mutilated body was found earlier that year.

1990 Beggs' conviction for murder quashed on a legal technicality.

1991 Beggs convicted for the attack on Brian McQuillan, which took place earlier that year.

1993 Beggs loses appeal against conviction for the attack on Brian McQuillan.

1995 Beggs released after time served for the attack on McQuillan.

1999 Beggs sought as prime suspect for the brutal murder of Barry Wallace. Flees to the Netherlands.

2001 Beggs extradited from the Netherlands. Stands trial later in the year and is convicted.

2010 Beggs loses final appeal against conviction for the murder of Barry Wallace.

1

Leap of Faith

There are almost always certain events in our lives which will have helped to shape the person we are or the person we will become. Some are as innocuous as that first kiss or a chance meeting; others are more defining, as in the birth of a child or the passing of a loved one. Whatever the event, the hope is that there is a positive that can be taken from it and built upon. In this story, however, for one man, that life-changing moment comes without any positives other than the realisation of just how close to death we can be at any time.

The man I met in London in September 2009 was not physically remarkable in any way – average, in fact, a quality that is preferable when one hopes to remain inconspicuous among the seven million or so other people living out the drama of their day-to-day lives in that city. But I already knew parts, at least, of the tale I was about to be told by this man, and I couldn't help but look at him in a different light; with a great degree of admiration for his courage and his conviction. He is without a doubt a born survivor, whose anger and frustration understandably turned into a near obsession with the man who almost robbed him of his life. His motives for telling his story are selfless, albeit cathartic for him, but clearly he sees it as his duty to warn people about this man he now knows so well; not so much a crusade on his part, but a cautionary tale for all.

The story starts with what would initially appear as a chance meeting between two strangers. There is nothing in his manner or conversation which would suggest that the man with the Northern Irish accent is anything other than an ordinary man in the street but, in truth, he is a cruel and sadistic killer who intends to lure his unsuspecting victim to his death.

The other man, a quietly spoken and inoffensive Glaswegian, has no idea that he has been singled out for slaughter. And, as he finds himself caught up in the bloody fantasy of a madman, he displays an almost superhuman determination to escape with his life, a decision which will count him among the most fortunate of people. Having survived what can only be described as a horrific ordeal, it is clear that there will always be many physical and emotional scars left behind for Glasgow-born Brian McQuillan. But, as those physical scars begin to heal, there remains a determination to understand how such a violent individual could have lived freely within a close-knit, quiet community, relatively free from scrutiny by police. For there was no doubt in Brian McQuillan's mind that, when he had looked into the eyes of William Ian Frederick Beggs one July night in 1991, he had been looking into the eyes of a killer.

***

To live every day of your life in denial would be an unimaginable existence for most of us. Knowing and accepting who and what we are, and fitting into society the best way we can, is what we do in order to remain true to ourselves. It is a reality which hasn't always been that easy to achieve though, bearing in mind the countless fears and prejudices which often have to be overcome. Those who reach adulthood today, however, do so in a more broad-minded society where enlightened attitudes exist because of the tireless campaigning and selfless sacrifice of others.

Rational, reasonable people accept that we are born into this world in various skin colours and with certain religious beliefs indoctrinated into us at a very young age, and that we can be attracted to people of the same or opposite sex. They also accept that, save being able to adopt a different faith if any to the one we are born into, it is impossible to deny our colour or our sexuality. In order to create the perfect society, we have to learn to live with each other and integrate as much as possible.

Living life as a Christian within a Church with a belief system anchored well and truly in the teachings of the Bible, while accepting your sexuality as that of a gay man, could be considered something of an anomaly. For 19-year-old Brian McQuillan, completing his probation as a youth worker within the Church of Scotland in a small parish in Dundee, it was anything but an anomaly. The young McQuillan was something of a militant in the sense that he openly challenged the Church on its viewpoint about homosexuality, and so his 'coming out' as a gay person was anything but a quiet affair. Adding further pressure to this was the fact that, at that time in Scotland, legislation regarding same-sex relationships was specific in that it was still illegal for two men to engage in sexual activity unless they were over the age of 21.

For Brian McQuillan, who was then entering into his first gay relationship with a man ten years his senior, there had to be a clandestine element to the affair. This was most certainly not by choice for the outspoken McQuillan, but more out of necessity, in consideration for the safety of his partner, who could have faced prosecution.

The early Eighties were a difficult period for a young man who was still a committed Christian and who had already mapped out a path in life, the route of which intertwined with that of the Church. It wasn't that the Church of

Scotland refused to accept homosexuals into their congregations. They were clear that everyone was welcome into their fold, but with the proviso that homosexuals remained celibate. This was a clear affirmation, in their eyes, of 'hate the sin, not the sinner'. It was obvious that a conflict of interpretation of the Bible existed between McQuillan and the Church and, for a period of a year or two, he resigned from its employ.

When he returned to the Church after his self-imposed sabbatical, he entered into a new position in a programme set up for drug rehabilitation. It wasn't long before his enthusiasm and commitment were rewarded and he was offered a senior position. Again, though, there existed a conflict for McQuillan. If he accepted this new position, he would have to commit to a positive, inclusive relationship with the Church and sign a declaration stating that he would remain celibate, a condition that was fundamentally hypocritical, as this declaration would not have been required if he had been a heterosexual male. Although still living in the same house as his long-term partner, the relationship between the two men had run its course, and he was, at that time, in a position to sign just such a declaration. He signed the document and immersed himself in his work.

The gay scene in Glasgow in the mid-Eighties was growing steadily and, as legislation was challenged and support groups increased, some of the fear felt by young men and women receded and certain clubs and pubs such as Squires and Bennets became synonymous with the GLBT (gay, lesbian, bisexual and transgender) community.

Brian McQuillan was introduced to Glasgow's gay scene through his long-term partner, but, rather than finding it safe and welcoming, he found it less than inviting. His recollections of it are as being 'cold' and 'frightening' on occasions, certainly not a 'community within a community', as many people would have believed it to be. Having met other gay friends while socialising with his partner, he tended to stay within that particular clique, with the people he already knew and trusted.

In early 1991, Brian had decided he needed to move out of the house he had shared with his ex-partner. They still had a solid friendship and there had been a lot of positives to take away from their time together, but Brian McQuillan saw this as an opportunity to spread his wings and experience life as a young, single male in a city with a vibrant nightlife and ever-changing attitudes.

After about six months, he found a comfortable flat to live in and settled into a new era in his life. It was July 1991, the Gulf War had dominated the news in the early part of the year, and Britain had sent its first woman astronaut into space. On the night of 11 July, Brian and a close friend called Malcolm had gone to an aerobics class after finishing work, and then back to Brian's flat. They had been out on the town together many times before, and had even travelled on a couple of occasions to Blackpool to experience the numerous gay clubs and pubs which had sprung up there in the latter part of the Eighties.

Back at the flat, both men drank for a while until just before midnight, when they decided, on the spur of the moment, to make a night of it and carry on to a nightclub. They had already shared half a bottle of whisky together and a couple of cans of beer, and were more merry than drunk when they arrived in Bennets a short time later.

As the night progressed and they worked their way through the club, Brian became aware of one particular male who kept smiling across the room at him. As he moved around the edge of the dance floor, this man would always appear close by and try to catch his attention. His demeanour was anything but threatening, and his smile was 'friendly', almost bold, but warm and engaging.

From what he could see, this man was on his own, but every now and again he would join up with a couple, a factor which Brian McQuillan later realised may have put him somewhat at ease, as it suggested he was known to others in the club. Even so, what did seem strange was the fact that, although he and his friend Malcolm remained at Bennets for the next couple of hours, the male never approached him to start up a conversation.

There was no instant attraction to this stranger whom McQuillan described as being of average height and build, but there was something about his eyes that were captivating. Copping off with someone was not anything either he or

Malcolm had planned for the evening anyway; they were there purely to dance and have a good time. In fact, McQuillan had only ever gone home with one man before, and that had turned into his first serious relationship, the very same relationship he had just recently ended. If anything, this man in the checked shirt and jeans who kept smiling over at him was forgettable, save for the fact that on the night he appeared to be omnipresent.

At closing time, around three in the morning, tired but now almost sober, both McQuillan and his friend left the club. Minutes later, Brian waved Malcolm off in a taxi and walked around the corner towards home. It had been a good night and, as both men had made a conscious decision not to drink at the club, McQuillan could look forward to the benefits of a hangover-free morning.

As he turned the corner, he was aware of a small, light-blue car, a Ford Escort, travelling slowly beside him next to the kerb. He could see the driver, and there was no mistaking him as the same male he had seen earlier in the club. As Brian McQuillan walked on a few yards, he came across the couple he had seen earlier with the male inside the club, and they were engaged in a full-blown domestic on the street. Instinctively, he stopped to intervene, and so, too, did the male driving the Ford Escort.

With the couple separated and sent on their way, both men stood together on the street and began to talk. It was general conversation, slightly guarded as in any first meeting between two people... until, that is, the subject of the Church came up. The male, who by then had introduced himself as Ian, professed to have strong links with the Church himself, particularly with the Boys' Brigade organisation. A commonality had been found.

After standing talking for a few minutes, Ian casually asked McQuillan if he wanted to come back to his flat in Kilmarnock and have a few beers, adding that he hadn't had anything to drink in the club on account of having to drive that night. Over the years, having worked with people with drug addictions whose only goal was to feed their habit whatever the cost, and who often displayed manipulative and deceitful behaviour in order to do so, Brian McQuillan believed he had acquired the skills which enabled him to have the measure of most people within a few minutes of meeting them. He was sure he could tell when someone was genuine or if they had another agenda. Here was a complete stranger asking him back to his flat for a drink at three in the morning, and the only signals he was picking up were that this was a warm and personable individual. No alarm bells were ringing and he felt comfortable enough to agree to get into the car.

They talked about all sorts of things on the 20-minute journey to where Ian Beggs lived at Doon Place in the Bellfield area of Kilmarnock and, when they arrived, Beggs showed McQuillan up to his first-floor flat.

Inside, it was sparsely furnished, clean and comfortable.

While McQuillan sat down in the living room, Beggs disappeared into the kitchen and came back into the room with a pewter tankard and a bottle of Grolsch beer, most of which he had already poured. Again, the conversation centred on Christianity and the Church, and particularly the Boys' Brigade. Perhaps it was the tankard from which he was drinking that was tainting the beer; he couldn't be sure, but Brian McQuillan found his drink had a bitter taste and he only took a few mouthfuls.

The topic of the Boys' Brigade kept coming up again and again throughout the evening, with Beggs insisting on showing his guest photographs of camping trips and outings he had been on with some of the boys he had mentored. For the first time that night, Brian McQuillan began to feel uneasy. There was something about his new friend that he couldn't quite put his finger on. Whatever it was, he was now sure he had done the wrong thing by coming back to the flat. As he became more and more aware that his host was now anything but the same person he had met earlier that night, his senses began to dull. It may have been the alcohol, but when he had left Bennets nightclub earlier he had felt sober enough, and he had only drunk a few mouthfuls of the beer Beggs had given him. Something else was happening.

Tired and listless, McQuillan told Beggs that he had to go to work the next day, and asked if he could have a blanket so he could sleep over on his settee. Although he still had this sense of dullness, he was clear in his thoughts that, regardless of what Beggs might have had in mind, he had no intention of anything physical happening between them. All he could think about was sleep.

It was much more than a normal sleep that Brian McQuillan fell into. Sometime later, he barely awoke into an almost incapacitated state, and he found Beggs had placed him on his back and had already removed most of his clothes. Beggs was attempting to pour more alcohol into McQuillan's mouth, the majority of which was running down his chin and on to his chest, soaking him. While he could see and feel all of this going on, he could not react to it in any way. There was no sense of the panic that there most certainly should have been, and there was no compulsion to push him away and flee. Even if there had been, his arms and legs felt heavy and cumbersome.

Beggs pulled his guest to his feet and led him into a small, single bedroom and told him to sleep on the single bed. Again, McQuillan felt himself fall into a deep sleep almost immediately.

When next he woke, he found himself on his back again, this time totally naked save for his socks, and he could see the top of Beggs' head at the bottom of the bed. It was a moment of total disbelief when he saw that his left leg had been raised off the bed and Beggs was doing something to it which he couldn't quite see.

Suddenly there was excruciating pain, and McQuillan's first thoughts were that he was being bitten. Without thinking,

McQuillan grabbed Beggs by the hair and yanked his head away. There was a look of sheer determination on Beggs' face, and a glimpse of something in his hand. Worse still was the sight of blood running freely from a deep wound in McQuillan's left thigh, the cut running the whole way around from back to front. There was blood absolutely everywhere. The bed was soaked, and both he and Beggs were covered in it.

Instinct allowed Brian McQuillan to push Beggs aside, leap out of bed and rush towards the living room. He felt totally vulnerable now, accentuated by his nakedness and the fact that he could see another laceration on his upper leg near his groin, which had probably happened as he had pushed past his attacker. There should have been pain, but adrenalin was now surging through his body, and every muscle was crying out for oxygen in anticipation of 'fight or flight'.

As he reached the bedroom door, McQuillan turned around to see where his attacker was. What he remembers is Ian Beggs, dressed in T-shirt and boxer shorts, standing facing him and holding his arms out to the side of his body. He appeared to be clutching something in both hands, between his thumbs and forefingers. There was an overwhelming sense of power emanating from Beggs, and a lack of urgency as he approached his victim, gently coaxing him to return to bed. As he neared, McQuillan raised his own hands and grabbed Beggs by the wrists to keep whatever he had in his hands at bay.

He could feel just how strong Beggs was, as now, locked in his grip, Beggs was pulling him effortlessly back towards the single bed. There was no emotion and surely no warmth in the eyes staring back at McQuillan. Beggs was unbelievably calm amid the blood and gore, all the time repeating that he should go back to bed.

All Brian McQuillan could think about as he fended off his attacker was the fact that no one knew where he was or who he was with. He hadn't even mentioned to Malcolm about the man who had kept smiling over at him during the night. He was convinced that he was about to die.

What he began to focus on then was a window which was just above waist height but was showing some daylight through the curtains. If he could only get to the window, or better still get through the window, he could, at least, attract some attention. At that moment, Brian McQuillan made a decision to jump through the first-floor, metal-framed window and take his chances rather than face this madman who was hell-bent on killing him. If he survived, then well and good, and if he didn't, then at least someone would find him and they would know what had happened to him that night.

Without another thought, Brian McQuillan headbutted Beggs, ran towards the window, covered his face with his right arm and dived straight through the curtains and the glass pane. Were it not for the fact that it had been raining all through the night, so that the grassy area below the window had been soaked and the ground softened, he may not have survived the landing. He fell 15 feet on to the ground and landed unconscious but in a perfect recovery position. He was alive. It was 9.30 in the morning on 12 July 1991.

From what he can remember, even though he had drifted in and out of consciousness, there was someone at his side almost immediately. His fall had been witnessed by a local man, Andrew Nimbley, as he went to get his car from a lock-up close to the flats in Bellfield. He remembered hearing a thud and the sound of glass breaking before he looked up to see a body plummeting to the ground. He recalled that the young man had a 6-inch-long gash at the top of his thigh and was covered in blood. The 57-year-old Mr Nimbley was obviously distressed but stayed with the man lying on the wet grass until help arrived.

Two of Beggs' own neighbours, William and Elizabeth Fisher, also went to McQuillan's aid, and they were struck by how terrified the young man had been, as he had been saying how he had to 'get away'. As luck would have it, a beat police officer had been only a few seconds away, and a female whom McQuillan only remembers as Brenda was there to give first aid from the outset.

Brian McQuillan lay prone, unable to move and speak, but fully aware of everyone fussing around him. Frighteningly, though, as his eyes moved from one person to another, among the people kneeling beside him, he saw the man who had just tried to kill him, now with a dressing gown covering his T-shirt and boxer shorts. There was no way for McQuillan to convey to anyone what had just happened but, equally, there were also too many witnesses present for Beggs to consider finishing what he had begun.

The next few hours saw McQuillan whisked away to hospital for emergency treatment, which in the end resulted in 26 stitches and a stay of five days. Apart from the wounds to his leg, he was battered and sore but, amazingly, no bones had been broken.

Police in attendance at the scene had immediately made the connection between the man lying soaked in blood on the grass and Ian Beggs, not least because it was easy to identify the broken window of his flat as being clearly where the drama had unfolded. While detectives waited to speak to the young man receiving treatment for his wounds, Beggs agreed to travel to the police station voluntarily, where he was able to give his account of what had happened.

The police were never in any doubt that Beggs had been the aggressor in the matter, yet, faced with the probability of serious charges being proffered against him, Beggs concocted his very own version of events in which he painted a picture from the outset of himself as the victim taking desperate measures to fend off a serious sexual assault on him by McQuillan. It would be discovered later that Beggs had used just such an explanation in relation to a previous incident, one which had had rather more serious consequences.

As Brian McQuillan lay in hospital over the coming days,

occasionally speaking at length with police officers who were investigating his case, he remembers quite clearly asking who exactly Ian Beggs was, and if he was known to police. A natural request after all, bearing in mind he had just escaped the clutches of this madman, and he found it unbelievable to think that Beggs had not done something similar before, such was the ferocity of the attack on him and the relative calm Beggs had displayed during the incident. He knew that there was more to this man.

The police, of course, were sympathetic towards McQuillan's request for information, but they first had to consider the restrictions of data protection. Their hands were tied in what they could reveal about William Ian Frederick Beggs' past, and they urged McQuillan to look towards the inevitable court case and to assist them in securing a conviction, which would probably see Beggs receive a custodial sentence. There was a certainty in the rhetoric the police used which in itself suggested to McQuillan that they knew Beggs very well, and that this was an opportunity which they were keen to take advantage of.

It would only be a matter of months, in October 1991, before Beggs would stand trial for the attack on Brian McQuillan, charged with the offences of assault causing severe injury, permanent disfigurement and danger to life. The trial took place at Kilmarnock High Court, and was relatively straightforward, lasting only three days, with the jury taking just 20 minutes to return a guilty verdict. For

McQuillan, though, having to stand in the box and face the man who had attacked him was difficult to say the least, but he confronted his fears and took a further step towards exorcising Beggs from his nightmares.

As would have been the norm, sentencing of the defendant was deferred to allow pre-sentence reports to be submitted to the court for consideration. There were, of course, concerns as to Beggs' state of mind, and whether he was or could be considered a danger to the public, and one of the necessary reports would include a detailed psychiatric evaluation.

Sentencing on the matter came at Edinburgh High Court about a month later, during which Mr David Burns QC, Advocate Depute (a public prosecutor in Scotland), informed the court that Beggs had two previous convictions for 'similar' attacks on men, a point which was not lost on Brian McQuillan, who was following the press reports on every aspect of the case.

After examining Beggs, Dr JA Baird, Physician Superintendent at the State Hospital, Carstairs, compiled a psychiatric report in which he came to the conclusion that Beggs had shown indications of a 'significant abnormality' in his personality. A further report had been compiled by Dr Baird at the request of the trial judge, with particular emphasis being given to whether Beggs could be considered a danger to the public, and whether the length of any detention could be left open, to be dealt with by continuing psychiatric evaluation.

The second report concluded that an indeterminate sentence would not have been suitable in Beggs' case, but the gravity of the crime itself would suggest a substantial term in prison. Counsel for Beggs, Ian Hamilton, was quick to point out to Lord Morrison that nowhere in a further psychiatric report, also compiled at the request of the court by Dr J McCurley, did it 'specifically state' that Beggs was a danger to the public.

In summing up, Lord Morrison concluded, 'There is a clear indication that you constitute a danger to the public and my first duty must be to ensure the public is protected from that danger.'

With great relief for McQuillan and the police team investigating the attack, Beggs was jailed for six years.

It should have been over for Brian McQuillan at this point. Justice had been done, and the man who had attacked him had been incarcerated. The pressures of giving evidence in an open court had been considerable and, as Beggs had persisted with his claim of self-defence against McQuillan as the aggressor, those pressures had multiplied. The issue in court throughout the trial had been one of credibility, but the physical evidence had been strong and McQuillan had proved a steadfast witness.

With all that seemingly behind him, it would be safe to assume that McQuillan would probably concentrate on trying to rebuild his life and leave the past where it belonged. But there were too many questions left unanswered. For McQuillan,

Beggs would never be confined to the past until he knew exactly who he was and what he had done before – and, more importantly, what he could be capable of in the future.

Even though the police had tried to convince him to move on from his experience, McQuillan refused to do so, and persistently contacted them, pressing them for information. The only advice he was given was that he should contact the Newcastle *Chronicle* and *Herald* newspapers and request any information they might have had on Beggs.

Over the coming weeks and months, armed with clippings from various newspapers, McQuillan was able to piece together the story of Beggs' life right up to the point where he had met him in Bennets nightclub. Every detail he uncovered only confirmed what he already knew in his own mind. The decision he had made to leap from that first-floor window had undoubtedly saved his life.

***

As a survivor of an encounter with Beggs, having looked him in the eye and witnessed at first hand the man behind the façade, Brian McQuillan knew that it would only be a matter of time before Beggs attacked again, and this time with more devastating consequences.

In December 1992, just a year after Beggs was sentenced at Edinburgh High Court, McQuillan felt compelled to write to newspaper editors with a chilling warning about the man he knew would be released from prison all too soon. He wrote, 'I am sure that I do not need to express the trauma I have faced since this assault and, more so, discovering this man's criminal past.' He then made reference to Barry Oldham, a young man whose name had featured in newspaper articles throughout the north of England just five years previously, adding, 'The largest part of my anxiety and sorrow is for the parents and friends of Barry Oldham, and if he [Beggs] is once again set free, most likely for his next victim.'

In May 1987, the mutilated body of a young man later identified as Barry Oldham had been discovered in a Yorkshire beauty spot. A murder inquiry was launched, but it would be nearly a month before William Ian Frederick Beggs would become the prime suspect.

2

Truth Will Out

Even though McQuillan remained resolute about uncovering the extent of Beggs' criminal past, reading article after article about the horrific murder of Barry Oldham was deeply unsettling. He admits to suffering bouts of depression and anxiety during that period directly after the trial, and finding it difficult to come to terms with things in general. The 'symptoms' he describes, should they be referred to as such, are classic in terms of a diagnosis of Post-Traumatic Stress Disorder (PTSD), but for him it was the tremendous feeling of guilt that overwhelmed him.

There is nothing new about the condition or syndrome which in the past has been dubbed 'Survivor's Guilt'. It has been recognised by therapists over the last 40–50 years as a condition often affecting those people who have survived traumatic experiences ranging from combat situations to major events such as the Holocaust in Nazi Germany during World War II. The sufferer would harbour strong feelings of guilt that they have lived through such events while others – relatives or friends perhaps – had not.

In more recent times, particularly during the devastating financial meltdown of 2008–09, there have been cases where the complainant has experienced this guilt if they have managed to keep their jobs when all around them colleagues have been laid off. This feeling of guilt, which will more often than not be accompanied by anxiety, depression, loss of sleep and social withdrawal, has since been redefined as another symptom of PTSD, rather than as a stand-alone condition.

As Brian McQuillan dug deeper into the circumstances surrounding the murder of Barry Oldham, the discoveries he made – rather than proving therapeutic in terms of confronting and moving on from the Beggs episode – only served to further reinforce his fears and uncertainty.

At around 9.00am on 12 May 1987, a gamekeeper, walking in the woods close to the scenic area around Clay Bank Top at Stokesley in North Yorkshire, discovered the mutilated and partially clothed body of a man. For the first few days of what was undoubtedly a murder investigation from the off, the victim remained unidentified. Within a week, though, police released the name of the dead man to the press as that of Barry James Oldham.

The nature of the wounds inflicted upon Barry Oldham and

the exact cause of his death were not released by the detectives at the time, but would be described later that year by pathologist Dr Michael Green during a subsequent trial. The victim's throat had been cut, probably from behind and, after death had occurred, the killer had tried to cut off the head and limbs. It was clearly a horrific attack, and one that few of the investigating team would fail to be repulsed by. With such a sadistic killer on the loose, time was of the essence.

The description of Barry Oldham and the clothes he had been wearing on the day he was murdered, which they believed to be the evening of 11–12 May, were released to the press in an attempt to jog the memories of the general public. The detectives involved in the case were now following a line of inquiry which focused their attentions on Tyneside, after discovering that their victim may have bought a bus ticket from Aberdeen to Newcastle on that day. They described Barry as being around 5ft 9in tall, 13 stone with thinning, light-brown hair cut short, and a light fair to ginger moustache. The clothes he had been seen wearing last were a grey checked sports jacket, with dark-grey trousers, a grey sweater, black shoes and a gold chain around his neck.

As each day would pass, the trail of Oldham's last movements would be getting colder and colder. Some of the most important breakthroughs in any murder investigation come within the first 48 hours, when witnesses are identified and crucial statements obtained. In this case, the police were already a week or so behind, and they were playing catch-up.

One other piece of information they did have, though, and were keen to release through the press in order to rule it either in or out, was the description of another male who had been seen alongside a brown-coloured Mini Clubman Estate car in the car-park area at Clay Bank Top, around the time the body may have been dumped. They described him as about 5ft 10in tall, about 30 years old, with an unkempt appearance and either a beard or very heavy stubble.

On 21 May, the *Journal* newspaper printed the sketched images of Barry Oldham alongside that of the person seen standing beside the little brown estate car at Clay Bank Top. They are contrasting to say the least, in that the unidentified male appears to be large in build with a dark and menacing demeanour, while the sketch of Barry Oldham portrays him as fine-featured and vulnerable. It was obviously not intentional, but already the images suggested that of a victim and his assailant.

The response to the crude image of Barry Oldham in the paper that evening was almost instantaneous and, before long, the investigation began to take shape and focus on the bars and clubs of Newcastle, a full 55 miles away from the site of the gruesome discovery. Police soon began to piece together the last movements of their victim.

The 28-year-old man riding the Northern Scottish bus from Aberdeen to Newcastle on 11 May 1987 was looking forward to a new job in an exciting new city, and another new start. By all accounts, Barry Oldham was a drifter, a free spirit who thrived on new experiences, and the promise of a job in a bar was enough to make him leave Aberdeen almost without thought.

Up until that day, he had been temping in telephone sales for Mercury Communications in the Scottish town, a job he had held for only a matter of weeks. For those who knew him well enough, he was openly gay, but not flamboyantly so, and he had a degree of talent as an artist; certain drawings of his adorned the walls of various pubs in the town.

It would be a laborious journey for Oldham, with the coach leaving at 9.30 in the morning, but not arriving at Gallowgate bus station in Newcastle until around 5.30 that evening. It was quite possible that he had made the journey before, as it transpired that there were extremely strong links between the gay communities of Newcastle and Aberdeen, with return trips having been organised from various clubs in both towns.

By all accounts, though, Barry James Oldham – or, as some had known him, Barry John Jackson, an alias he had used more than once – was no stranger to travel. Originally from Bolton in Lancashire, Oldham had only been living in Aberdeen since the Christmas of 1986, having worked in Jersey throughout the rest of that year. But he had already travelled extensively in Europe and America, and had held down a number of different jobs including salesman, barman and even a position as a croupier at one point.

When he stepped off the bus at Newcastle, Oldham stored

his luggage in a locker at the station and made a phone call to a friend in Aberdeen to say that he had arrived safely at his destination. He then phoned the person he had arranged to meet in relation to the promise of a job, and he was told to make his way to the Courtyard bar in Marlborough Crescent in the town, where he arrived at around 6.00pm.

He was met there by the friend who had promised him a job – Billy Blanchflower, or 'Hetty' as he was more commonly known. There were a few other males in their company, and they all remained there drinking for a couple of hours. After leaving the Courtyard, they went off to a private address in the West End of the city before eventually returning to the centre and, in particular, a renowned gay club called Rockshots in Waterloo Street. The club was known to be busy most nights of the week, and police became convinced that it was the place where Oldham first came into contact with his killer.

As a joint inquiry team made up of detectives from North Yorkshire and Northumbria Police eased themselves into a hastily prepared incident room at Newcastle's West End Police Station, Detective Superintendent Robin Cooper, the then Deputy Head of North Yorkshire CID, urged revellers at the club to come forward with information, promising strict confidence.

There had been some solid identifications of Oldham made by one or two patrons who had been at the club that night, and even a suggestion that he had been intoxicated, spilling his drink and even falling asleep at a table during the evening. His behaviour was apparently what had drawn their attention to him, but there was little else they could offer. One witness had come forward to say that they believed Oldham had left the club alone at around 1.00am, but police had thought that unlikely bearing in mind the time frame of when they believed he had been murdered.

In many ways, Rockshots was proving the worst of places for police to canvas for witnesses to come forward with information relating to the victim's movements. Even though there were thought to have been at least 300 people at the club that particular night, the response they were getting was poor. This was not surprising in that many of those at the club that night could ill afford to be caught up in what was rapidly becoming a high-profile murder investigation.

There were those in the gay community who had a perception of the police as nothing more than homophobic thugs, and more than a few of the club's patrons were hiding their true sexuality amid heterosexual relationships, and feared the consequences of being 'outed'. This mistrust and open hostility was proving difficult to get past.

Whatever the reasons, Detective Chief Superintendent Tony Fitzgerald, the head of North Yorkshire CID, and the man leading the murder hunt, decided to go public on 26 May and renew an appeal for more witnesses to come forward. To press the message home, he warned the public – but particularly those within the gay community – that the killer could strike again. At that stage, the police had failed to establish a motive for the slaying, but there was the distinct possibility that Oldham had been targeted because of his sexual orientation. In his statement to the *Evening Chronicle*, Fitzgerald warned, 'It may have been just a homosexual meeting that went wrong, or it might be someone who bears a grudge against homosexuals. If that is the case, others may be at risk from this killer.'

There was a sense of frustration apparent in the words and phrases being used, but more obvious were the underlying threats that police would not be content with the limited assistance they had been given and were prepared to probe deeper in an attempt to identify the majority of the 300 or so who had been there that evening. To put further pressure on the club owners to assist, Fitzgerald promised that, if it was deemed necessary, police would be extending their interviews into the Rockshots club's members list, which totalled in excess of 35,000 nationwide.

Without going into any detail, Fitzgerald suggested that someone could quite possibly be shielding the killer, adding, 'The injuries to Mr Oldham were such that there must have been a lot of blood around at the murder scene and in the vehicle which brought the body to North Yorkshire.'

He didn't have to paint a picture for anyone in respect of the severity of the injuries to Oldham. The newspapers had already used adjectives such as 'mutilated', 'brutal' and 'vicious' in reporting the story, but Fitzgerald was determined to emphasise just how dangerous the perpetrator was to any member of the public.

There were other aspects to the investigation which the inquiry team decided to share with the press in an attempt to either firm them up as solid leads or scratch them out as dead ends. On discovery of Barry Oldham's body on 12 May, the crime scene directly around the remains had been searched extensively for any trace material which may have been left by the killer or killers. During that search, a silver Zodiac ring in the form of a scorpion and bearing the inscription 'scorpio' on the rear had been found about 10 yards from where the body lay. It was quite possible that the ring had been there for some time, having fallen off the finger of a rambler in the area, but until the owner was identified it could not be ruled out that it may have belonged to the killer.

One other development which could have been coincidence but had to be pursued was the fact that, on 6 May, just five days before Oldham arrived in Newcastle, a brown-coloured Mini Clubman Estate car had been stolen from the Metro centre in Gateshead and remained listed as missing. This, of course, was the same model and colour of car seen at 7.30am at Clay Bank Top on the morning of 12 May. The registration of the stolen vehicle was given out as DLG 484S, and police reiterated just how important the car might prove to be in the investigation.

It was clear at this point, in and around the end of May and the beginning of June, that more details of Barry Oldham's injuries had either been leaked to the press officially or unofficially. By now, the *Evening Chronicle* was aware that the killer or killers had unsuccessfully attempted to dismember the victim's arms and legs and speculated that this may have been an attempt to fit the body into the rear of a car, quite possibly the little brown Mini Estate.

What had to be considered by police was the possibility that Oldham may have been murdered somewhere in Newcastle city, and the body transported the full 55 miles to the secluded beauty spot in order to throw investigators off the trail and buy the killer some time. It was plausible in the sense that the dump site for the body was devoid of any signs of a struggle or large deposits of the victim's blood, and the manner in which Oldham had been murdered and mutilated would have suggested that forensic evidence would have been present there if it had been the original crime scene.

Intelligence gleaned from the few gay men who had come forward had suggested that a popular meeting place for gay liaisons in Newcastle city was the gardens area at the rear of St Nicholas's Cathedral down towards the Quayside. Search teams from the SPG or Special Patrol Group had carried out fingertip searches of the bushes and shrubbery in that area looking in vain for a crime scene or the victim's missing clothing.

The investigation was being pulled in several directions, each lead proving just as fruitless as the next, but one constant still remained. Somewhere amid the hundreds of people who had attended the club on the night of 11 May was potentially a solid witness who could provide a key piece of evidence which might lead them to the killer.

Yet another appeal by Detective Superintendent Cooper printed by the *Evening Chronicle* on 28 May displayed further signs of frustration. 'Unfortunately we have had a disappointing response from the gay community. We want them to know that we are not concerned with their homosexual activity but we want them to come forward in strict confidence with any information about Barry Oldham's movements that night.'

Bearing in mind the nature of the assault on Barry Oldham, police had to consider the possibility that the killer(s) had murdered before, or that they had been involved in other crimes of violence, and the murder had been an escalation in their offending. Working on that theory, they had engaged several of the team in cross-referencing similar offences throughout the north of England, in which the attacker had used knives or blades to inflict injuries on his victims.

As they continued to search through databases and liaise with other constabularies, one member of the public in particular was already making a connection between himself and the circumstances Barry Oldham may have found himself in on the evening of 11 May.

It may have been something which 51-year-old retired

school teacher Hugh Marr wanted to put to the back of his mind for many reasons, but he couldn't help but wonder if the man who had attacked him after a night at Rockshots nightclub could have been capable of killing someone. Whatever the risks, he was prepared to approach police and give them details of an incident which had occurred in February that year, in which he had been attacked and slashed after being given a lift home from the club by a male with a Northern Irish accent who had said he was a student at Middlesbrough Polytechnic. The incident had happened at Marr's home in Tyneside and, at the time, he had decided not to report it to the police.

It wouldn't be long after that before the inquiry team had identified that student as William Ian Frederick Beggs.

There was another person who thought she recognised the person depicted in the photo-fit image being shown on local television broadcasts. In fact, she had been sitting beside this man when the image had flashed up on the screen. It immediately occurred to Lucinda Geldard that her friend and fellow student Ian Beggs was a perfect match for the man seen at Clay Bank Top, both physically and in the other details that were released, particularly the link to a small brown estate car. When she had an opportunity, she contacted police and told them of her suspicions.

It would be 1 June before Detective Sergeant Charles Day would interview Ian Beggs in relation to his movements on the evening of 11 and 12 May. At the time, Beggs had been living in digs in Princes Road in Middlesbrough, a 40-mile journey for the detective, during which he must have wondered if anything positive would come from the interview.

It was anything but promising when Beggs said that he had been at home studying on the evening of 11 May, and, when shown a photograph of Barry Oldham, he responded by saying that he had never seen the man before; even more so when Beggs admitted that he had frequented Rockshots nightclub in the past, but not for some time. He told Day that the last time he remembered being there was with a friend from Northern Ireland called Robert Lyle, who had been over in Newcastle on a training course.

Beggs insisted, however, that, despite being an occasional patron of the club – one among many, as he pointed out – he was not in any way a homosexual. Possibly on realising his protestation might be taken as a display of outright homophobia, Beggs added, 'But the idea does not bother or concern me.'

It was clear that DS Day placed some importance on these statements made by Beggs, as he saw fit to note them down and refer to them later when the matter came to trial. During the investigation, all manner of motives had been considered; among those, of course, was the possibility that the killer was a violent homophobe. It certainly wasn't a crime for a heterosexual male to frequent one of the biggest gay clubs in the country, but it was unusual; and his denial that he was homosexual had seemed a little incongruous for someone who surrounded himself with gay men. Even the physical similarities between Beggs and the description of the man seen at Stokesley would have been hard to ignore, and may have rung alarm bells for Day.

Over the next two days, a culmination of further enquiries and discrepancies in Beggs' first account made DS Day return to Princes Road to speak to the young man again on 4 June. Beggs had fled and, according to a friend, had shaved his beard and drastically altered his appearance. These actions alone were enough for police to seek a search warrant in relation to the flat and alert surrounding constabularies to the possibility that a killer was on the run.

The follow-up search of the flat at Princes Road on 5 June revealed substantial traces of blood – which were later to be matched forensically to that of Barry Oldham – and other trace evidence which would tie the suspect to the murder. But without their suspect in custody, no amount of forensics would bring the team any closer to closing the case.

As the Scene of Crime Officers worked away collecting their samples and labelling them for submission to the laboratory, the inquiry team were feverishly rooting through documents at Beggs' flat in an effort to narrow down where he might have gone to ground. It wouldn't be long before they knew the address of the Beggs family's home in Northern Ireland, and that Beggs himself was the registered keeper of a brown-coloured Mini Clubman Estate, the car which they now believed he had driven up to Scotland and then across on the ferry to the port of Larne. This was the first real break, and they were confident they had identified and were in pursuit of their prime suspect.

3

Close Shave

On 6 June 1991, what would have been shaping up to be a normal Saturday duty for Royal Ulster Constabulary Detective Sergeant Andy Sproule proved to be anything but when he was briefed by Chief Inspector Drew Clint at Lurgan Police Station, in reference to the circumstances surrounding the murder of a man at Stokesley in North Yorkshire. He was told that there was a possibility that the prime suspect in that case was currently at a dwelling just outside Moira, a few miles down the road.

Along with him in the CID office, making notes and waiting for the final signatures on a search warrant, were Detective Constable Hamilton and Detective Constable Bob Kinnersley, both experienced in dealing with matters of serious crime. The telephones had been ringing all morning with arrangements being made between the RUC and Tony Fitzgerald of the North Yorkshire Police as to how matters would progress should the arrest be successful.

To a large extent, the operation went without any great fuss. On their arrival, the police were admitted to the house and Beggs was arrested by Andy Sproule almost immediately. He seemed neither surprised nor particularly fazed by the event, although his family had a wholly different reaction, one of total disbelief. As far as they were concerned, the whole thing was one huge mistake, and their son could not have been involved in anything criminal, never mind murder.

The search of the house continued, and during that search a tent was seized for examination, as was a brown-coloured Mini Clubman Estate car.

There were very few seasoned detectives or uniform officers working in the Royal Ulster Constabulary during the 1980s who had not witnessed or played a part in the investigation of various atrocities during the darker days of the 'Troubles'. The area around Armagh, Portadown, Lurgan and Craigavon had seen its fair share of paramilitary murders and attacks over the years, with the perpetrators, if caught, commanding very few column inches in the newspapers. Murder was a word much bandied about, used almost without thought for the enormity of the crime it described or the devastating consequences it had for the victims' family and friends. But, as each episode of violence was in some way upstaged by another more horrific, callous and indiscriminate act, the police, and the public for that matter, could not help but become slightly desensitised. It might have been a consequence of the belief by many on both sides of the political divide that casualties were to be expected in times of conflict, and that there would always be a certain amount of collateral damage in terms of innocent bystanders becoming victims.

But all of a sudden there was the emerging story of Barry Oldham's murder, which, although it had happened on the mainland, was now in the local press after the arrest of a possible suspect just a matter of miles from Belfast. As the story unfolded in the newspapers, it seemed to strike a chord with the greater Northern Ireland public. It wasn't so much the macabre nature of the murder, with the victim's throat having been cut and the subsequent attempt to dismember the body, although such gruesome details always titillated. It was more the fact that the prime suspect was a County Down man from a respectable Baptist family, who had connections, however tenuous, with Northern Ireland politics. It was that hint of scandal touching upon the middle class, God-fearing, Unionist, mid-Ulster community that probably gave the story some legs over the coming days and weeks.

The sullen-faced, unkempt Beggs, who had not made a reply to the caution he was given by DS Andy Sproule, was driven away and lodged in a cell at Lurgan Police Station. When the good news was relayed to the inquiry team in

England, four men began their car journey to Stranraer in Scotland to catch the first available ferry to the port of Larne in Northern Ireland. Detective Sergeant Charles Day, and Detective Constables Simpson, Woodhall and Sanderson had been tasked to fetch the prisoner and return with him to Tyneside along with the little Mini Clubman Estate and any other evidence found in the search of Beggs' family home in Moira.

It was a Saturday night by the time they arrived and any return travel arrangements had to be scheduled for the next morning. Their counterparts in the RUC had thought ahead and had already arranged lodgings at the White Gables hotel in Hillsborough. Some of the team from Lurgan CID, including Sproule, met with them at the hotel and a few pints were had and a few stories exchanged. There was always common ground between police officers, regardless of jurisdiction, and the consensus among them all was that Oldham's murder was one of the worst they had come across.

The next day, a Sunday, DS Day took custody of Beggs from Lurgan RUC and was driven to Aldergrove Airport, where he and one of the detective constables accompanied their suspect on a flight to Manchester. On arrival at Manchester Airport, their plane was met on the runway by a police car, and they were all transferred to Richmond Police Station. Throughout the journey, Beggs had been constantly reminded that he was still under caution for the murder of

Barry Oldham, and that any statements he made may well be used in evidence. DS Day would later give evidence that during the car journey to Richmond he had witnessed Beggs become upset and close to tears at one point. He stated that Beggs was asked why he was upset and whether it was because he had been responsible for Oldham's death, and that Beggs had replied, 'Yes.'

As Beggs was accepted into custody at Richmond and faced a long series of interviews regarding the murder of Barry Oldham, the brown Mini Clubman Estate was being driven off the ferry at Stranraer and towards the forensic laboratory at Wetherby in West Yorkshire.

At last the pace of the investigation was moving up a gear. The prime suspect was in custody and both the physical and circumstantial evidence was accumulating and being assessed in terms of the weight it would carry during any subsequent court case. As in any major investigation, all the 'i's had to be dotted and the 't's crossed; procedures such as the continuity of exhibits and the gathering and interpretation of forensic reports had to be strictly adhered to. The very notebook entries made by those members of the team who contributed to every aspect of time-lining the movements of both victim and perpetrator were checked and collated. Statements from witnesses and police officers alike were typed and checked for errors and checked again. With all the exhibits either photographed or bagged and labelled, the team were ready to interview their suspect.

Any investigation, but particularly one as weighty as a murder inquiry, relies very much on how experienced the interviewing officers are and how much preparation they have put into their interview plan. Modern approaches to interviewing have identified that there are two very different agendas during the questioning, one being that of the suspect and the other, of course, the police. How the police interview plan is laid out can affect the overall outcome. The so-called PEACE model has been in use for some time by most constabularies in the UK, an acronym describing the various considerations: Preparation and Planning; Engage and Explain; Account; Closure; Evaluate.

In the planning stages, the interviewing officer has to consider the possible answers or explanations the suspect will provide to relevant questions they are asked, and be ready to rebut those answers. Every possible excuse or denial has to be challenged with either physical evidence or circumstantial reasoning, placing the suspect on the back foot and negating any possible defence. As with any offence, there are points to prove, and many of the questions will have to centre around those points until the police agenda has been met.

The suspect will be given the opportunity to account for their movements on or around the time of the offence, and provide an explanation, if any, for their involvement in that offence. At the start of the interview, they will have been reminded that they are under caution, and that in layman's terms the essence of that caution means that during the interview is the most appropriate time for them to give an explanation for their involvement in an offence. Should they fail to do so, but later, in court perhaps, they provide a wholly different excuse or explanation, then that court will draw its own inferences from that failure. In very simplistic terms, the suspect's defence could possibly be damaged by their reluctance to provide police with a full and frank explanation at the earliest possible time, i.e. during the interview.

There will have been a period of consultation, of course, between the suspect and their legal representative prior to interview, and they will have been advised what and what not to say. Therefore, their account of events is revisited again and again during the interview to check for anomalies and inconsistencies, and a final account of the events is agreed. A successful result for police at the end of the interview is to have asked all the questions they require an answer to, and for the suspect to have provided an explanation of events, one which they intend to provide to the court, and, in this case, the jury, as their defence.

The evaluation of the results of that interview are crucial, particularly in a case involving a murder. The suspect may need to be interviewed on several occasions in order to clarify matters further or on the basis that the first or subsequent questioning has identified further offences or other evidence has come to light.

Regardless of the fact that this investigation took place

back in 1987, there would still have been a plan as such to the approach taken by the inquiry team in relation to the series of interviews. But it is clear that their suspect, Beggs, had already decided on the explanation he was going to give police, a story which he would use as his defence when faced with the charges of attacking Brian McQuillan years later.

According to Beggs, on the evening of 11 May, he had indeed gone along to Rockshots nightclub, and he had met Barry Oldham by chance. He stated that Oldham had told him he had nowhere to stay that night, having only just arrived in Newcastle, and Beggs agreed that he could spend the night in his flat. For some reason, when they finally returned to Beggs' flat in Middlesbrough, Beggs claimed that Oldham decided they take a tent and camp out. The spot they supposedly camped out at was close to Stokesley, Clay Top Bank, to be precise.

Sometime during the night, Beggs claims that he woke to find Mr Oldham assaulting him in a sexual manner. He described Oldham as being a lot bigger than he was, and holding him tightly. It was at this point, according to Beggs, that he remembered having a razor blade in his wallet, and he told Oldham to stop what he was doing or he would use it. When he didn't stop, Beggs said that he was able to reach the razor blade and slash Oldham across the arm. The assault apparently didn't stop at that, and Beggs said that he was forced to keep lashing out at him with the blade.

There was blood coming from Oldham's arm, and Beggs explained that he had attempted to give him some first aid by taking off his own shirt and wrapping it around the bloody wound. That was as much as he could remember at the time, as he stated that he had then blacked out. When eventually he came to, he said it was daylight, and he tried to rouse the figure lying beside him. He said that Oldham was out cold but, on turning him over, he saw the wound to his throat and the realisation that he was dead sent him into a blind panic. In that panic, he admitted to having tried to dismember the body but, when he couldn't quite manage it, he abandoned the remains close to the campsite.

Throughout his interviews, though, there was a common denominator. At every opportunity, Beggs was clear that he was not a practising homosexual, and that he was not in the habit of picking up gay men for sex or any other gratification. In his own words, he said of homosexuality, 'I find it repugnant, but, as far as other people are concerned, it's a matter for them.'

As each day passed, though, the case against Beggs was building and, as it was now clear they had their man, the inquiry team were checking on Beggs' background and any friends he may have had either at Teesside Polytechnic or back in Northern Ireland. Gradually, they were piecing together a picture of the suspect – his lifestyle, hobbies, associations and, of course, his sexual orientation.

The Royal Ulster Constabulary were still very much

involved in the case in that DS Andy Sproule had been interviewing anyone who could enlighten them as to who the real Ian Beggs was. In the week after he had arrested Beggs in Moira, he had spoken to his old headmaster at Friends School in Lisburn and had travelled to the coastal town of Bangor to speak with a man called Robert Lyle, whose name had come up during one of the interviews with Beggs.

As with the other people the police had spoken to who had known Beggs for some time, Robert Lyle was taken aback when he was told the nature of their enquiries. He wasn't able to shed much light on Beggs' past other than what he knew from their shared interest in politics, particularly the Young Conservatives. He was able to confirm, however, that, while he had been on a course in England, he had made contact with Ian Beggs, and they had both gone out one night to Rockshots nightclub. In his recollection, though, he described the whole idea about going to a gay club that evening as being innocent enough. Beggs had told him that a lot of the students at Teesside would frequent the club, not because of their sexuality, but just for a few laughs, to experience the 'gay scene'. Nevertheless, regardless of what little he could provide them in terms of background on Beggs, Robert Lyle would find himself being called as a witness during the trial in subsequent months.

Even though the police had convinced Hugh Marr to make a statement of complaint against Beggs in relation to the assault in February, they had more good news in the form of three further complaints by students Simon Williams, Simon Robinson and David Lawrence that they, too, had been attacked by the same man in similar circumstances.

When Hugh Marr recounted his story to police, he was open and honest about his sexuality, and told them he regularly visited gay clubs and bars. He had met Beggs on a Saturday night out at Rockshots in February that year, when this man with the Northern Irish accent had offered him a lift home. According to Marr, he invited Beggs into his flat and then into his bed, and Beggs did not decline. As far as Marr was concerned, he expected to have consensual sex with Beggs, and described how he initiated the approach. 'I touched him with my hand two or three times, and he did not respond, so I turned over and went to sleep.'

Sometime during the night, though, Charles Gray, Mr Marr's flatmate, heard a commotion and his friend's voice crying out. When Gray reached the bedroom, he saw two men naked on the bed with a stranger 'pinning' his friend down. Mr Gray later testified that Marr had pleaded with him to 'get this idiot off me'. As Beggs stood up, he complained to Gray that he had cut his thumb and asked for an Elastoplast. It was Marr, however, who had sustained two cuts to his back, and was bleeding. After Gray handed Beggs a plaster, he left without any further incident.

It was a compelling story, and all sorts of scenarios must have been going through the minds of the senior investigating officers. Had, for instance, Beggs been involved in murder before and Marr just had a lucky escape, or had they managed to catch a serial killer in the making? When they heard the accounts given by the three other students, none of those scenarios seemed far-fetched.

According to Simon Williams, he had been in student accommodation alongside Beggs, when one night he had awoken to the sensation of something or someone cutting his left shin. What he saw was a razor blade lying near him, and Beggs fleeing back to his own room.

The story told by Simon Robinson was similar, in that he had moved into a flat which Beggs already shared, and sometime in November 1986 Beggs asked him out for a drink. On their return, Robinson professed to feel ill and went to bed. When he woke the next morning, he found that he had a cut just above his left ankle, which later became infected and needed hospital treatment. He asked Beggs if he knew how he had sustained the cut, but he said that he did not.

When student David Lawrence was given some of Beggs' home-brew beer and became drunk, he had to retire to bed to sleep it off. He, too, awoke to find he had been cut on the leg. In this case, however, he had sustained a 5in wound which had bled out considerably and needed 13 stitches to close.

With such overwhelming evidence presented to them that William Ian Frederick Beggs had a history of preying on men, particularly gay men, and wounding them with a blade as the weapon of his choice, the team had to consider charging him with all four offences of wounding, alongside the murder charge. In many ways, it made sense in that they would be able to establish a pattern of behaviour which had undoubtedly escalated to the point of the vicious and calculated murder of Barry Oldham, whom many were describing as 'the perfect murder victim'.

Up until that point, all the people Beggs had allegedly attacked had been too close to home, each of them living either in multi-occupancy residences or in the very same property as Beggs himself lived. It would have been almost impossible for him to escape detection in those circumstances. But Barry Oldham had presented himself as the perfect choice. He had just landed in Newcastle that day, was clearly drunk and possibly incapable of rational thought, and had few if any real friends in the town. It was quite plausible that Beggs had quizzed Oldham about his circumstances and, if so, he would have gathered that Oldham was a bit of a free spirit – travelling around both home and abroad, taking casual employment when and wherever he thought to stop long enough. Very few people, if any, knew where Oldham was going, and it was likely he wouldn't be missed for some time.

On 10 June 1987, Beggs appeared at Stokesley Magistrates' Court charged with the murder of Barry Oldham on or about 12 May, and with maliciously wounding Hugh Marr sometime between 31 January and 1 March of that year. For the time being, those charges alone were enough to hold him in Durham Jail on remand.

4

The Case Is Opened... and Shut

It would be December of that same year, 1987, when Beggs would stand trial for the murder of Barry Oldham at Teesside Crown Court. As in any murder trial, it was expected there would always be media interest, but from day one the press were reporting on the minutiae of the proceedings. The fact that Beggs had attempted to cut off the head and limbs of his victim was always going to appeal to the sensationalists, but there was an added element to this crime which stretched out the column inches.

As they had done when details of the murder first emerged in May and June of that year, newspaper headlines still seemed to focus on the homosexual angle to the story. It was as if the fact that both the victim and possibly the perpetrator were gay added extra value to the perceived depravity of the crime. One has to remember that attitudes towards homosexuality in the Eighties were far from enlightened, and anything other than heterosexual relationships were still considered by many to be abnormal. There was also considerable focus in the media given to the emergence of HIV/AIDS, and concerns over how rapidly the disease was being spread were at their highest in 1987.

A publication on behalf of the Scottish Government in 2006 in relation to changing attitudes towards discrimination over the years cited 74 per cent of people surveyed in 1987 had felt that sex between people of the same sex was 'always' or 'mostly' wrong. That is a staggering statistic, regardless of how much emphasis we put on opinion polls and whether the people surveyed represented a fair cross-section of the general public. Any changes in attitudes would only happen gradually as subsequent generations adopted less blinkered, more progressive viewpoints than their parents or grandparents. Still, even five years on, in 1992, the British Social Attitudes survey recorded a tally of 58 per cent in respect of the same question asked in 1987.

Bearing these facts in mind, when reading from the newspapers at the time, one might be forgiven for thinking that Barry Oldham was the architect of his own demise, simply because he was a gay man. Had he been straight, of course, he would never have been anywhere near Rockshots nightclub, and therefore never in harm's way. Whether we agree or not, there was a perception then, and there possibly still is, that the lifestyle shared by gay men is one which would naturally attract violence; it is often portrayed as a seedy and perverted underworld of promiscuity and debauchery. This view is, of course, ignorant, narrow-minded and inaccurate, but such attitudes feed off the type of sensationalism that the tabloid newspapers churn out day in, day out, making it all the more difficult to counter.

Barry Oldham, a man who had been slaughtered at the hands of a cold-blooded killer, deserved to be treated as any other victim of crime would have been, in a sensitive and compassionate manner. Whenever possible, though, it appears the papers concentrated on his sexual orientation, and not Barry Oldham the son or brother or uncle; what they succeeded in doing was almost dehumanising him in the eyes of their readers.

For example, in the *Evening Chronicle* printed on 11 December of that year, Oldham is described as Beggs' 'bleeding homosexual victim'. It is wholly unnecessary to include the word 'homosexual' in that sentence. If Oldham had been straight, they surely would not have called him Beggs' 'bleeding heterosexual victim'! But would the same article have had the required effect if they had just described him as the 'bleeding victim'?

The jury of six men and six women charged with the job of reaching a verdict in the case of William Ian Frederick Beggs would have to listen to a considerable amount of evidence presented to them by the prosecution team led by

QC Steven Williamson. The basic facts as far as the prosecution were concerned were that, on or around 11 or 12 May that year, Beggs had met up with Barry Oldham at Rockshots nightclub in Newcastle and, after befriending him, returned with him to his flat in Middlesbrough, where he murdered him and tried in vain to dismember his body. Realising that he could not successfully do so, Beggs transported the body in his car to a place near Stokesley where he dumped the remains. They would attempt to prove that Beggs had a history of violence, all of which involved cutting his victims with blades or knives, and was, himself, a sadistic homosexual.

In answer to the prosecution case, the defence, led by James Chadwin QC, would say that Beggs had indeed met Oldham at Rockshots nightclub, and had camped out with him that evening at Clay Bank Top at Oldham's request. During the course of the night, Oldham had tried to sexually assault Beggs, who had lashed out with a razor blade in self-defence, causing Oldham a mortal wound. When waking the next morning and realising that Oldham was dead, Beggs panicked and tried to dismember his body.

For Brian McQuillan, who was reading about Beggs' self-defence claims in these same newspaper articles some five years later, it was all too familiar. The issue in his own case had also been one of credibility, with Beggs claiming that McQuillan had been the aggressor, and that Beggs had caused him injuries while fending him off.

Only the killer himself would be able to say if Barry Oldham had known much about what was happening to him the night he was murdered. According to certain witnesses who had seen Oldham in the club that night, he had been heavily intoxicated and, if that were the case, his senses may have already been dulled to the point where he was oblivious to what was happening. But one person who knew more than anyone what Barry Oldham may have experienced was Brian McQuillan, the man who had looked the killer in the eye and lived to tell the tale. Were it not for his own actions on the morning of 12 July 1991, he, too, may have made the columns of the Scottish press as the second victim of a gay serial killer. A chilling thought, and one which he would reflect on for some time to come.

For the defence, it was imperative that they convinced the jury that Beggs was heterosexual. If they stood any chance of adding credibility to his claim that he had been defending himself against a sexual assault by Oldham, then he would have to be seen to be straight and an unwilling participant. There was the possibility, though, that by doing so they could lead the jury to draw the conclusion that Beggs was, in fact, a violent homophobe who preyed on homosexual males. Either way, it was a fine line, and one which required them to character-assassinate Barry Oldham, painting a picture of him as an aggressive homosexual who had a predilection for importuning male victims.

In due course, Beggs would testify that it was Oldham who

had suggested that they camp out that evening. Again, this was an important element to the game plan in the sense that it implied that Oldham had been the more dominant of the two, and may have been in a fit state to make decisions and possibly devise a plan for assaulting his new friend. In addition, the spontaneity of the incident during a spur of the moment camping trip would remove any aspect of motive, a very necessary element in proving premeditated murder. They would also argue that the reaction of Beggs to finding Oldham dead that morning was naturally one of blind panic and self-preservation.

It would be a difficult defence to maintain, however, considering that the prosecution had lumped four other slashing attacks in with the murder charge, and that one of those victims, namely Hugh Marr, would give evidence that would further cast doubt on Beggs' heterosexual claims.

The prosecution were sure that they could prove that Beggs had the means, motive and the opportunity to carry out this heinous crime, and they intended to prove beyond doubt that he was a gay man who had an unhealthy fascination for cutting people. To give some background to the man sitting in the dock, the Crown had called witnesses who either knew Ian Beggs well, or had met him in one fashion or another; each of them recalled disturbing incidents where they had felt threatened or uncomfortable in his presence.

On 11 December, a musician, appropriately named

Johnny B Good, who had caught the Larne to Stranraer ferry in late May and decided to hitch the rest of his journey, explained how Beggs had offered him a lift after he, too, left the ferry in his car. Not only had he offered him a lift, but he had also plied him with drinks and a meal, and then offered him a bed for the night at his flat. During the night, however, Mr Good stated that he woke to find the zip on his sleeping bag had been partially undone, and Beggs was standing beside him dressed only in his underpants. At this point, Mr Good said that he believed that Beggs was a homosexual, and was making advances, so he packed up and left the flat. It was possibly a little light relief for the jury in terms of testimony, in that Mr Good was obviously a colourful witness. There was a sinister element to his story, however, as it had allegedly taken place only a fortnight after Barry Oldham's body had been found, and a matter of days before police first interviewed Beggs. If the dates had indeed been accurate and the story factual, then it had to be considered that Beggs had possibly been looking for his next victim, and Mr Good had been fortunate to escape.

Another acquaintance of Beggs, Joseph Hughes, who had originally met him on a visit to Rockshots, recalled how they had both watched a video film which he had described as 'horrific', but which Beggs had seemed to find funny. The plot of the film involved two men who met with and then murdered a homosexual man. According to Hughes, it was graphic in nature and he stated, 'It was horrific. I couldn't watch it. I like horror films but this one was too much. Ian seemed to find it funny. He said he had watched it a couple of times before.'

Taking everything into consideration, it would have been difficult for any juror to ignore the fact that Ian Beggs spent a reasonable amount of his spare time in one gay club or another, and that in doing so it was also reasonable to assume that he was gay. The prosecution was at pains to point out that Beggs was actually a full member of Rockshots nightclub and, by all accounts, a regular visitor there, regardless of the fact that he had to drive 40 miles from Middlesbrough to get there.

As far as the prosecution were concerned, they believed they had done enough to dispel the myth the defence had tried to create that Beggs was as straight as the next man and as much a victim as Oldham was in this unfortunate series of events.

The question of exactly where the murder had taken place was also of the utmost importance to both legal teams. The defence would have to prove that the camping trip had actually taken place and that the events, which they considered had been instigated by Oldham, had happened inside the tent. The situation that Beggs had then supposedly found himself in the following morning, and his subsequent panic, meant that he had simply abandoned the body close to the area where the tent had been pitched. They had to convince the jury that there had been no premeditation on

Beggs' part, and that his acts were those of an innocent man caught up in a nightmare scenario.

Of course, the prosecution totally dismissed that version of events, and the wrangle continued throughout the trial. The fact that Beggs had taken Oldham back to his room, a place which was private and away from prying eyes, and that Oldham had been drunk and possibly incapacitated, provided Beggs with both the means and the opportunity to carry out his deed. It was hard to deny.

The story about camping out was unlikely to say the least, and even unlikelier when one considered the timeline of events. If Beggs had met Oldham in the club sometime late that evening, as he had said, and had then driven 40 miles to Middlesbrough to his flat, and then another 15 miles to Stokesley, it would have been sometime in the early hours of the morning before they would have arrived at the campsite. Then there was the issue of pitching a tent in the dark. There were just too many holes in Beggs' story for any reasonable person to believe it.

Just as damning, however, and much more compelling evidence for the jury to consider was that given by pathologist Dr Michael Green. When he appeared in the witness box on 14 December, he was clear that, of all the injuries Oldham suffered that night, the fatal injury was the wound to his neck. He described how he believed the assailant had possibly held his victim's head back and cut his throat from behind, leaving a wound measuring 4in across which had not cut his windpipe, but had cut through the jugular vein on both sides of the neck. With such an injury, he believed death would have been rapid once air had reached the victim's heart. There were other smaller cuts around the neck, much less severe, but all of which would have happened when the victim had been alive.

As if that alone was not convincing enough, he catalogued the other cuts, starting with the 7in slice on Oldham's right elbow, which ran from side to side and had been deep enough to reach the membrane covering the bone. Alongside this wound and running parallel with it had been what he described as four 'tentative cuts'. Across on the left elbow he had found a lesser cut about $3^1/_2$in in length but only reaching superficial muscle. The cut to the right knee was, however, fairly substantial, measuring a full 12in from side to side and so deep that it revealed the end of the thigh bone. On the left leg he had found a smaller wound about 9in in length. In his opinion, the cuts to the legs and arms had been administered after death.

Throughout his evidence, Dr Green was adamant that he considered none of the wounds to have been in any way random, stating that in his examination he found them to be in symmetrical groups. He was also clear that there would not have been great blood loss during the attack, possibly as little as a pint and no more than two.

All the more frightening was the fact that he had not found any signs that the victim had been rendered unconscious before the attack by either a blow to the head or something of that nature, but the fact that he had consumed alcohol that evening may have left him in no position to defend himself.

There was no need for clarification for the jury. It was clear that the wounds inflicted on Barry Oldham had been done so in a calculated and almost methodical manner, and had not, as the defence had suggested, been the result of Beggs lashing out wildly with a razor blade. No murder weapon was ever presented to the court, but Dr Green had suggested that a sharp knife had been used to make the fatal neck wound. So, if the jury had to consider that the attack on Oldham was deliberate, then it was also likely that the murder had taken place in Princes Road, and the body moved later on the morning of 12 May.

Defence counsel James Chadwin was quick to place doubt in any juror's mind, though, by suggesting that the amount of blood found at the defendant's flat by the forensic team had not been consistent with the estimate given by Dr Green. He went on to say that, when the tent which had been seized had been examined, there had been signs that considerably more blood had been shed inside it and on the flysheet. Mr Chadwin also referred the jury to one of the police interviews during which Beggs had openly admitted to washing the tent and sleeping bags at Teesside Polytechnic laundry after the murder to get rid of the blood.

Of course, the other explanation for the traces of blood inside the tent was that Beggs had used it to wrap Oldham's body in and transport it out into the countryside. It made perfect sense. The tent was roomy and designed to keep out the elements, particularly moisture. What it could keep out, it could also keep in.

To add further credence to that explanation was the amount of blood that was found inside the little Mini Clubman Estate car. That particular piece of evidence had already been presented to the court earlier in the trial, when the judge, Mr Justice Staughton, all 12 jurors, barristers and the defendant himself had gathered in the court car park, where the car had been brought as the largest of all the physical exhibits. Before they left the court, prosecuting QC Steve Williamson asked the jury to pay particular attention to the luggage area, the back doors and the space inside. The defence counsel asked the jury also to look at the space between the seats.

The purpose of the exercise was, as far as the prosecution were concerned, to show that there was enough space in the rear of the car for the body to have been transported from Middlesbrough to Clay Bank Top, which would have explained the traces of the victim's blood found inside. The defence were less clear about why they had asked the jury to consider the space between the seats. The explanation they would give for the blood in the car, however, was that it had been released from the tent and the missing clothes when they were being transported away from the area where Oldham's body had been found.

THE CASE IS OPENED... AND SHUT

On 15 December, the prosecution team were dealt a blow as Justice Staughton directed the jury to find Ian Beggs not guilty in respect of wounding Hugh Marr, although the charges of assaulting the three other students – Williams, Lawrence and Robinson – were still before the court. It wasn't a disaster by any means, but it did help to concentrate their minds on the real job in hand, attaining a conviction for Oldham's brutal murder. Everything else they were prepared to sacrifice.

On Friday, 19 December, after both the defence and prosecution had given their closing arguments, and Justice Staughton had completed his summing up for the jury, a guilty verdict was returned for the charge of murder and for two of the counts of wounding. The regional newspaper, the *Journal*, reported the court's decision in brief and that a life imprisonment sentence had been handed down to 24-year-old Ian Beggs, for the murder of Barry Oldham. Just a week before Christmas, Beggs had to try to come to terms with spending the next 15–20 years of his life in prison.

5

Human Rights and Wrongs

There was little doubt in anyone's mind, least of all the members of the jury, that a fair and true verdict had been reached at the end of the trial. The idea that Beggs had acted in self-defence was not credible and the evidence to support a conviction for murder was compelling. A guilty man was behind bars, and the inquiry team could take credit for having conducted a thorough investigation.

It was expected, of course, that Beggs would seek grounds to appeal and, just as soon as the verdict had been reached and the life sentence handed down, he began to put those wheels in motion. The grounds upon which Beggs' legal team were eventually granted leave to appeal were that the original trial judge, Justice Staughton, had allowed the jury to hear evidence of the defendant's bad character, which in their opinion would have tainted any decision relating to the murder charge.

It would be the beginning of 1990, only two years after the original trial, when the decision would be taken to quash the conviction, and Beggs walked free from the court. What had happened to make the Court of Appeal judges rule in the appellant's favour?

During the trial, the prosecution presented accounts of previous razor attacks on men carried out by Beggs. Bearing in mind that Barry Oldham had had his throat cut by a razor blade, the jury would have found it difficult to ignore the fact that Beggs' 'bad character' – i.e. his previous offending history with a similar weapon proved he had a propensity to such violent behaviour – and was likely to have committed this act. The appeal was successful purely on this point of law, and the evidence as such – physical, documentary and circumstantial – was of no consequence in the decision-making process.

In 2003, the Criminal Justice Act made fundamental changes to the admissibility of 'bad character' evidence in matters before the court. The rule excluding evidence of a defendant's disposition to commit the offence for which they were being prosecuted was once described by Lord Sankey as 'one of the most deeply rooted and jealously guarded principles of our criminal law'.

There were inconsistencies and over-complications in its use, and such cases as Beggs' successful appeal would be cited as one of the reasons for consideration for reform some 13 years after his release for the Barry Oldham murder.

As far as Brian McQuillan was concerned, the law, in particular the judicial system, had let him down just as much as it had Barry Oldham. It is hard for any of us living in the free world to argue that, as part of our democratic rights, and in keeping with Article Six of the European Court of Human Rights, one should not be entitled to a fair trial. It is generally accepted that if we believe in the rule of law then we must abide by the decisions made by those chosen to preside over the adjudication of the law. It can be a bitter pill to swallow on occasions.

For Brian McQuillan, it was understandably more difficult to accept that Beggs could have been released on a technicality, leaving him free to attack again just over a year later in 1991. Under the terms of the European Court of Human Rights, both Barry Oldham and Brian McQuillan, although having been subjected to torture and inhumane treatment, had not had their human rights either engaged or breached. The terms state that it can only be a 'State Party' – i.e. a police force or government body, as such – which can be held accountable for breaching one's human rights. But if we look at the success of Beggs' appeal for the Oldham murder based solely on a technicality, the introduction of 'bad character' evidence during the trial, with no consideration given to the forensic and circumstantial evidence in the case, one can argue that that decision did not fulfil the obligation as set out by the European Court of Human Rights in that 'there is a positive duty to prevent foreseeable loss of life'. It must have been considered at the time of the appeal that Beggs presented a potential risk to the general public and, in quashing his conviction, the appeal judges had to know that they could be placing another person's life in danger.

With the judges having ruled in Beggs' favour at his appeal, one must ask the question as to whether Barry Oldham, the victim, had received justice – a 'fair trial' under Article Six. Did Brian McQuillan himself, as a result of that decision, have his rights under Article Three, which prohibits torture, taken away? The only winner was Beggs, who had been afforded all the consideration of a legal system which many have suggested weighs heavily in favour of the criminal.

On his release from prison, Beggs considered his position with regard to continuing to live in the north of England. The Oldham murder had been a high-profile case from the outset, and too many people in the gay community, not to mention the North Yorkshire Police and those on Tyneside, knew Beggs by sight and reputation and knew exactly what he was capable of. In order to start afresh and further cultivate his penchant for violent attacks on males, he had to move out of the area.

That same year, in 1990, Beggs moved to Kilmarnock in Ayrshire, setting up home in a flat at 2b Doon Place, in the

Bellfield area. Sometime prior to his move, possibly while still in prison, Beggs forged a number of references, citing his work on a Master's thesis which he had supposedly carried out and, on the strength of that, secured a position as a housing estate management officer with the Kilmarnock and Loudoun District Council.

Now he had a job, a place to live, and he was within 20 minutes of Glasgow and the gay clubs and pubs dotted around the city. Beggs now began to create his new persona, one which was both convincing and disarming and which would allow him to continue living his double life. Over the next year or so, he was to become a regular at Bennets nightclub, and it was there that he would trawl for potential victims.

Whatever his reasons for doing so – be they cathartic, therapeutic or sheer bloody-mindedness – Brian McQuillan had managed to put together every piece of the puzzle which was Ian Beggs, right up until the point in time when he himself had become another one of his victims. Everything he had believed he had seen in the eyes of the man who had attacked him had been there, and more. There was, however, no comfort in knowing that he had been right all along. If ever he could be sure about just how close he had come to death, he could be sure now.

Perhaps in itself that realisation compounded the feelings of anxiety and stress, all of which would return shortly when he received news from the investigating officers in his own case; Beggs was to appeal against conviction and sentence. While McQuillan had been picking through back copies of the newspapers in the north-east of England, making connections and circling dates and details, Beggs had also been busy poring over court transcripts and consulting with legal counsel in an attempt to tease out plausible points on which to seek appeal.

It shouldn't have been a surprise to anyone when Beggs launched his appeal against conviction and sentence just six months after the trial. He had nothing to lose after all. He had been successful before in his appeal in the Oldham murder, and from that had gleaned enough of an insight into the criminal justice system and all its flaws to consider the possibility that he could once again find a loophole to exploit.

The appeal was initially launched on four grounds, each of which the appellant claimed would equate to either misdirection by the trial judge or a miscarriage of justice. On the first count, Beggs claimed that the judge had provided the jury with examples of the evidence which had been put forward by the Crown, which went towards corroborating McQuillan's version of events. The judge had informed the jury, during his directions to them prior to their deliberations, that they had to consider other factors when determining the credibility of McQuillan's story, and not just his testimony alone. He went on to explain that the fact that McQuillan had thrown himself through the window could have been, as had been suggested by the Crown prosecutor, the actions of a person being attacked rather than those of an aggressor. The judge had also reminded the jury that the Crown's case relied on the nature of the wounds inflicted upon McQuillan, and that it would be up to them to determine how and in what circumstances they believed those wounds had been caused.

Another plank of Beggs' appeal alleged that there had been a further miscarriage of justice in that the judge had failed to put Beggs' case of self-defence adequately to the jury. In short, the appellant considered that the judge had spent more time concentrating the minds of the jury on the complainant's case than on his defence. He believed there had been no references made to the injuries he himself had sustained at the time of the incident, particularly the blow to the forehead. In truth, the police surgeon who had examined Beggs after the event was only able to find what he described as a small laceration on his left eyebrow.

Finally, Beggs referred to an issue relating to evidence given by two police officers, namely PC Dyer and Sergeant Steel. In his grounds for appeal, he stated that there were differences between details in PC Dyer's notebook and his statement, which was in the form of a transcript during the trial, and that any statements Beggs gave to Sergeant Steel, which had been admitted in evidence during the trial, had been made voluntarily and not under caution. He stated that he had gone along voluntarily to the police station with Steel to help them with their enquiries, and therefore had not been considered as a suspect.

The first date for the appeal hearing came on 28 May 1992 and, not surprisingly, Beggs had decided to represent himself in the matter. Immediately upon arriving in front of the judges, Beggs sought an adjournment so that a police notebook could be examined by an independent forensic expert. In Beggs' opinion, he considered that the typewritten transcript of handwritten entries in the police notebook relating to what he had said in an interview had been fabricated. He also stated that the handwritten entry in the police notebook was not an accurate account of that interview.

After deliberation, the appeal panel decide to grant an adjournment until a future date, but pressed the appellant to lodge the issue as a further cause for complaint to add to the existing four grounds of appeal. They were very clear in that they would be unable to consider new evidence relating to that matter unless this was done. They also suggested that Beggs seek the advice of experienced counsel to help develop the point and, in light of that, should apply for legal aid.

Although Beggs had displayed a certain arrogance by both representing himself and introducing an issue for consideration so late in proceedings, he did take on board all that the panel had suggested and, on 5 June, the Scottish Legal Aid Board wrote to the Clerk of Justiciary informing him that aid had been granted for the appeal.

A full six months later, on 7 January 1993, Beggs

appeared before the Appeal Court with his counsel Mr McBride. Again, there was an application for a further adjournment in order for the notebook in question to be attained for examination. For the notebook to be released, an application had to be made to the court, as it was in the custody of the court, having been produced at the original trial. Up until that point, no application had been made. In fact, a photocopy of the notebook entry had been supplied to Mr McBride on 16 September 1992, which in itself may have provided them with enough time to lodge such an application.

With their patience already tested, the judges agreed to adjourn but only until the next morning. They insisted that Beggs' counsel draft and lodge a further justification for appeal with an affidavit from Beggs stating the information on which this was based. The next morning, Beggs' affidavit was submitted to the court, taking issue with the notebook entry having been fabricated, information which he suggested he was not aware of until after his conviction.

The matter of the entries in PC Dyer's notebook had been made an issue backed up by a report supplied to Beggs by handwriting experts Dr Malcolm Coulthard and Dr Peter Finch from French Associates in York. It was Beggs' parents, William and Winifred, who had first engaged the consultants on their son's behalf, still clinging to the belief that the police had yet again made a terrible mistake.

In Beggs' opinion, there were discrepancies between the

notebook and the typed transcripts, which amounted to clear indications of tampering. This, of course, was only Beggs' interpretation of the report, and, when the appeal judges read it for themselves, they could not find any such suggestion.

When Beggs' counsel was informed that the Appeal Court was not going to order the release of the notebook, Mr McBride offered no further argument. What happened next was no surprise either. The appeal judges were informed by McBride that, after he had discussed issues relating to the four remaining matters with Mr Beggs, the appellant had wished to continue by representing himself. Mr McBride was given leave to withdraw from the appeal.

When Beggs had finished arguing each of the remaining four grounds, the panel withdrew to consider the issues. They returned to inform the appellant that they had refused the appeal against conviction, and that matters in relation to his appeal against sentencing had then to be considered. All that Beggs could offer in this matter was an opinion on the psychiatric reports, which had been prepared by Dr JA Baird, in that he believed them to be inaccurate and based on innuendo. It was an altogether amateur attempt at challenging the findings that Dr Baird had arrived at, even more so when he misinterpreted the report penned by Dr J Curley of Dykebar Hospital, a report which Beggs' own defence counsel had referred to during their plea-in-mitigation.

The appeal panel found Beggs' comments unhelpful and of

no consequence when considering the term imposed upon him. In fact, they considered the trial judge had acted in the defendant's favour when, on consideration of the reports, he chose not to impose a life sentence for what was effectively a very serious assault with aggravating factors. His appeal against sentence was also refused, and the six-year term stood.

The police had been vindicated and the integrity of the justice process in this case was preserved. To say that it came as a relief to McQuillan that the appeal had fallen through would be an understatement. But he wasn't the only one who had concerns about Beggs being released from prison. The neighbours who had lived beside him in Doon Place had approached the council in an attempt to have Beggs evicted from his flat in his absence, on the basis that many of them now knew as much about his past as McQuillan did. In their opinion, if released, he could present a danger to the public at large, and could be a disruptive element in what was a quiet residential estate. Within a short period of time, though, it became apparent that Beggs and his immediate family had managed to secure the property for his return, having negotiated its purchase after a lengthy legal battle.

There was absolutely nothing anyone could do to prevent Beggs from setting up home in the very same place where he had attacked Brian McQuillan. When he was eventually released and returned there permanently, he installed cameras and a security system at the flat. His neighbours were convinced, though, that the cameras were there for the purpose of spying on them rather than protecting the property.

Although Brian McQuillan had endured much since the attack in 1991, he had made great efforts to move forward and normalise things in his life. Relocation out of Glasgow to the small town of Maybole on the Ayrshire coast was part of that plan. Although only a 30-minute drive away, the bracing sea air and small-town mentality was a welcome break from the pressures of city life.

But there was also no hiding from the fact that Beggs would be released from prison at some stage and, taking into consideration the time he had spent on remand awaiting trial, as well as the remission he was due for good behaviour, he would serve only three years of his six-year sentence. As Beggs had tuned into the gay scene in Glasgow, chances were he would return to the places he had known and frequented, and it was likely their paths would cross.

That day came sooner than McQuillan thought it would, but not where he had expected it. On driving back from Glasgow one evening sometime in 1995, just a few miles out of Kilmarnock, a car a short distance ahead of him and travelling in the same direction drew his attention. There was something familiar about it, something which made him speed up slightly and close the gap between them. And, as he drew closer, he knew by the make and model and the distinctive Northern Ireland registration that it was the car which Ian Beggs had picked him up in three years earlier.

The two cars continued on for a few minutes, with McQuillan registering the shape and outline of the driver as being that of Beggs. As if realising the scrutiny he was under, the driver of the Ford Escort began to stare intently into the rear-view mirror, and for both men there was a moment of recognition. Surprising himself, McQuillan followed the car as it drove into the car park of Ayr swimming pool, and watched as Ian Beggs got out of the car and strolled across towards him. When he reached McQuillan's car, Beggs bent down and looked in the windscreen and grinned before walking off and going inside the complex.

He may not agree with me, but, as Brian McQuillan told me this story in 2009, I detected a real sense of anger and frustration. Unconsciously, he had balled his hands into fists, his knuckles whitening. I believe from the moment he recognised the details on the number plate, McQuillan had wanted Beggs to know he was travelling behind him. He wanted to confront this man, to let him know in no uncertain terms that he was not afraid of him, and that he had regained control over his life; that he was no longer a victim. It was an exercise in facing up to his worst fears, and part and parcel of the continuing process of empowering himself. He did admit that at the time he had wanted to drive his car over the top of Beggs as he walked through the car park, but common sense prevailed.

Not long after the incident, the local police paid a visit to Brian McQuillan's home to make enquiries into an incident of criminal damage caused to a motor vehicle belonging to William Ian Frederick Beggs outside his flat at Doon Place. The accusation was that McQuillan had deliberately targeted Beggs' car sometime after their meeting on the road. Even today, some 15 years later and with Beggs locked up in prison for the foreseeable future, Brian McQuillan denies taking any such action.

If only we could be afforded the opportunity to go back in time and speak to those people who had the misfortune to come into contact with Ian Beggs up until 1995, and seek their opinion as to whether they considered him a danger to the public, I am in no doubt that their answer would be that he was and always would be. It was never a matter of *if* he would ever attack and hurt anyone again, rather a case of *when*. Unfortunately, it wouldn't be that long at all before the beast would raise its head again and prove them right.

6

Loch Holds the Key

There are few places in the British Isles which come close to matching the beauty and tranquillity of Loch Lomond and the Trossachs National Park. The loch itself is vast, almost 25 miles long and 5 miles across at its widest point, and reaching depths of over 600 feet. Dotted with around 60 lush green islands, many of which are thought to be crannogs (artificial islands built by settlers in prehistoric or medieval times), the loch straddles the Highland Boundary Fault, marking the gateway from the lowlands of Central Scotland to the Highlands.

To reach the loch from Glasgow is little more than a 40-minute car journey, but the change in the landscape is nothing less than a total transformation. One cannot help but be moved by the serenity of the place, particularly on a clear, calm day, as the fresh, crystal-clear waters lap gently against the rocky shores. It is hard to imagine how anyone could desecrate such beauty, but that is exactly what Ian Beggs did when he dumped the body parts of his next victim in shallows at Rowardennan, on the east side of the loch.

The challenges that face any emergency services' underwater diving team can be numerous as their duties require them to assist in both search and rescue operations, carried out more often than not in difficult and demanding environments. Thorough and repetitive training exercises help to both reduce any potential risks and fine-tune skills. The Central Scotland Police Underwater Unit based at Stirling trained regularly in Loch Lomond; the great depths and variety of obstacles which the natural topography of the loch bed provides lends a degree of difficulty to various training scenarios. But, on one such exercise in early December 1999, the team couldn't quite believe what they had come across.

It was 6 December, the waters were icy cold and the first of the divers, Mark Westmorland, was working in a depth of around 15 feet near to Balmaha pier. There was always a certain amount of debris floating just on or below the surface of the loch, whether it was rotting pieces of wood or vegetation, or discarded rubbish thrown in by inconsiderate tourists. But there was something more sinister inside these bin liners that the diver grasped with his gloved hand. When he brought the first bag to the surface and opened it, one can only imagine his reaction when it revealed a severed human hand. In the other bag there was a foot with part of the leg still attached.

Instinctively, the diving team moved from training to operational mode, and it wasn't long before there was another find. Another limb, this time an arm with a hand attached, was brought to the surface, and then on the next day a human thigh. It was clear from what they had found up to that point that the body parts probably belonged together, and that they were not looking for more than one victim. It didn't lessen the horror of the discovery, though, and the police officer appointed to take charge of the case, Detective Superintendent Douglas Neilson, told the press that police were checking through missing persons files in an attempt to identify the victim whom they knew to be a male.

It would be another ten days before the remaining leg and foot would be recovered, but there was still the matter of the torso and, crucially, the head. At the early stage of the recoveries, all the police were willing to speculate on was that the victim was between 18 and 40 years of age, and that the killing could very well have been gang related. The search itself was extended to include the land running alongside the area where the first discoveries had been made, and police on the ground were aided by a police helicopter. There was every expectation that the rest of the cadaver would be found in the same area.

All throughout the weekend of 11 and 12 December, as

families up and down the country made their last preparations for Christmas and what was promising to be a huge Millennium Hogmanay celebration, police in Central Scotland and neighbouring constabularies were poring over missing persons reports of males fitting within the age range they had identified. That initial estimation was to change, however, when, after examining the remains at length, a forensic anthropologist working for the police narrowed the age range down to between 20 and 25 years. He was also able to say that the male would have been around 6ft to 6ft 2in tall.

The age and general description of the as-yet-unidentified murder victim did fit reasonably well with a young man by the name of Barry Wallace, who had been missing since the morning of 5 December. It was an unpleasant task but necessary when the police approached the Wallace family to inform them of the discovery and advise them that at a later stage they might be asked to provide a sample of DNA, in order to rule out the possibility that the remains were those of their missing son. Mr Ian Wallace, Barry's father, gave a statement to the press which was more of an appeal for his son to return home than a consideration that the gruesome discovery in Loch Lomond could be in any way connected to his absence. In that interview, he stated, 'They [the police] have spoken to us and are 99 per cent certain that the body in the loch isn't Barry because they think it has been there for a while.'

Looking at the timeline involved, it is easy to see how Ian Wallace would have dismissed the idea as being out of hand. The police diving team had found the remains in the loch on Monday, 6 December, and at that stage Barry had only been missing for one day after failing to return from a Saturday night work's party in Kilmarnock town. There was no way this was his son. As far as he was concerned, Barry must have had other reasons for not wanting to come home, and he was determined to find him and deal with whatever issues were keeping his son from the bosom of his family.

It's a natural reaction for someone to dismiss the worst possible scenario and continue to believe that all is well, even when there are details which suggest otherwise. Without tangible and undeniable proof, we will cling to the only other rational explanation, that it is someone else's misfortune, someone else's son or daughter lying in a refrigerated tray in the morgue waiting for their family to be told the awful news that no parent ever wants to hear. It is surely one of the worst duties for a police officer when detailed to deliver a death message to the relatives of the victim of a sudden death or fatal road crash. There is never an easy way to tell anyone that their loved ones have passed away, but often the presence of a uniformed police officer walking up the path towards the front door is enough for some to realise their worst fears. I have witnessed people closing the door in my face, as if by preventing me from telling them the inevitable truth this will change the reality of the situation. If they didn't actually hear the words, then everything was all right. Although Ian Wallace had been told that the body parts recovered from the loch had been there for a while, and were therefore unlikely to be connected to his missing son, there must have been that feeling of awful dread still lingering in the back of his mind. What if this *was* Barry?

As DNA comparisons continued on the severed limbs, and the search at Loch Lomond proceeded relentlessly, a possible development came to light some 60 miles away and a full ten days after the first discovery. A woman by the name of Margaret Burley had been walking her dog on Barassie Beach at Troon on the Ayrshire coast when she noticed a plastic carrier bag lying just above the high-water mark. There was a rip in the side of the bag through which she could see what looked to be a human head. A retired doctor, Dr Graham Mann, who was alerted to the find looked inside at what he first thought to be a wax model, only to realise that it was a severed head. His examination was brief, but he did offer an opinion that the head was that of a dark-haired male between 20 and 30 years old. Having lived and worked in the area, and having walked the beach regularly, he considered that the bag and its contents had been dumped there, as he believed the location where it was found, high above the high-tide mark and almost in the grass, would never have been reached by incoming tidal waters.

The beach was subsequently sealed off by police, and the head was taken to the morgue to enable tests to begin to establish any links to the severed limbs. Door-to-door enquiries were made and an appeal launched for anyone witnessing suspicious activity in the area of Barassie Beach to come forward with information.

Regardless of how noncommittal the police remained when asked to comment on whether the head actually belonged to the other body parts already found, the press had already made the connection and again it was the name Barry Wallace which featured in news reports.

With the local and national newspapers running the gruesome murder story on their front pages, and a growing atmosphere of fear developing within the community, the police eventually confirmed that, after DNA comparisons had been made, they could be sure that both sets of dismembered remains, the limbs and the head, belonged to missing Kilmarnock teenager Barry Wallace. It was devastating news for the Wallace family, and worse still for Ian Wallace when he was asked to formally identify his son's remains. One can only imagine the distress he must have felt when he gazed down at all that was left of his beautiful boy.

For the police, though, there was more than one issue to contend with. They now had a grieving family, a general public convinced there was a maniac on the loose and a timeline of events that so far stretched over ten days. Additionally, there had already been two crime scenes, Loch Lomond and Barassie Beach, but it had been established that neither was the scene of the actual murder. And, crucially, they had no suspects – or did they? Knowing Barry's last movements had been in his hometown of Kilmarnock, the police had to consider that the suspect came from the same general area.

As the story developed in the media, as it was bound to do bearing in mind the horrific nature of the crime, one man reading the newspapers and catching the odd television bulletin at his home in London had already decided who the killer was. According to Brian McQuillan, there could only be one person living in the Kilmarnock area who was both capable of murdering and then dismembering a young male victim, and likely to do it. After all, he had nearly succeeded in doing so before. There was no mistaking it: Ian Beggs was the man the police should be looking for.

There was no satisfaction for McQuillan, having already warned whoever would listen some seven years previously that Beggs would strike again, but there was frustration. After all, it wasn't as if the local police didn't know who Ian Beggs was and what he had been convicted of in the past. As one source inside the police was to say, 'When William Beggs' name is tapped into the police computer, it should light up like a Christmas tree.'

Of course, the impact on McQuillan, should his suspicions prove to be accurate, would be much more than frustration. Having tried to erase Beggs from his mind, relocating hundreds of miles away from friends and family, he was possibly just beginning to rid himself of his spectre.

But, in truth, he was never more than a nightmare away from seeing Beggs' face as he walked slowly towards him with his arms outstretched, urging him to come back to the blood-soaked bed in the little bedroom in Doon Place.

It was now Friday, 17 December 1999, two days after Barry Wallace's head had been found on the beach at Barassie. At this stage, it was clear that the senior investigating officer, Detective Superintendent John Geates, had now identified Ian Beggs as a potential suspect and had put the wheels in motion to detain him and carry out a search of his property. Throughout the early hours of the morning, search teams were assembled, briefed and then deployed at the flat in Doon Place as close to first light as was possible.

During the briefing, it would have been pointed out exactly what items had been recovered along with the body parts and the head, which may or may not be pertinent to the search. One of those items was of particular interest. The bag in which Barry Wallace's head had been found was a branded Scandinavian Seaways carrier bag, particularly distinctive and not something that would be found in every household. As the police were looking around the outside of the flat, they came across bags of rubbish piled up, the contents of which suggested that someone had been decorating. One officer on closer inspection recognised the logo on a bag as being identical to the one described during the briefing. The significance of the find was considerable, and the search immediately stepped up a gear.

Neighbours confirmed that they witnessed numerous police officers force entry into Beggs' flat that morning, and then over the next few hours a steady stream of police came and went and removed a number of bags, which they assumed were evidence bags, from the property.

Scene of Crime Officers were in attendance almost from the outset. It was obvious from what they found inside the flat that it could well have been the crime scene which they were desperate to identify and contain. But, crucially, there was no sign of Ian Beggs. It had to be considered that he had already fled, knowing full well that he would have been the first port of call for police in a crime such as this committed in the general area. Immediately, they began to canvas neighbours living at Doon Place about the single man living in 2b.

Although Beggs had now been living in Kilmarnock for nine years, albeit three of which he had spent in prison, the local police had not been keeping particularly close tabs on him. The fact that they were not able immediately to identify a place of work for Beggs, and then move towards detaining him there as soon as it was discovered he was not at his flat, makes it clear that it is likely that the police had no reasonable, up-to-date intelligence on Beggs.

Police forces across the UK, and, for that matter, around the world, rely on the intelligence that is fed into their systems by the ordinary officers patrolling the streets in order to create a database of offenders in their area. It is expected that police officers, working in various communities, will become acquainted with personalities in those area, particularly people who would be considered repeat offenders and, after time, they should eventually be able to recognise them on sight. It is also expected that, if they do recognise someone they believe to be of interest, they will submit an intelligence sighting to their criminal intelligence officer or whatever equivalent title that particular constabulary or force has adopted for that role. Some of the detail on these intelligence reports could be as simple as the clothes the person was wearing at the time they were observed, who they were with and their exact location. Whatever those details are, though, that sighting is logged on the police computers and, when that individual's name is recalled, a full profile of the person can be viewed. By creating an intelligence picture of an individual, the police will be able to keep themselves, and their officers on the ground, up to speed on any vehicles, associates, clothing, addresses and indeed occupations which may be relevant to that person. Regular stop-checks on that person might reveal yet more information about their day-to-day movements; if and where they are working, perhaps, or if they have settled into a relationship with someone and might be cohabiting at an address police might not have linked them to before.

Today is the age of intelligence-led policing. But that intelligence does not necessarily need to come from police officers alone. A great source of information is the general public; people living and working in the community who unwittingly pick up little snippets of useful intelligence and then pass that information on to police. They may not appreciate the relevance of their contribution, and will possibly never know how significant it proves to be if at all, but it may very well be the last little piece which fits into a much bigger jigsaw.

The neighbourhood police officers working in and around Bellfield in Kilmarnock could and should have been the conduit for collecting information from the residents in that area. But it was soon apparent to constables knocking on the doors either side of Beggs' flat that not only did his neighbours know quite a bit about the habits of their strange neighbour, but that they had also already expressed concerns about his comings and goings. The Strathclyde Police must accept that at some point there appears to have been a breakdown in communication between themselves and the local community. I am not suggesting for one moment that this was a failure on the part of the community officers alone. But the question has to be asked as to what emphasis Strathclyde Police placed on Beggs being a potential danger to the public, and what steps they took, if any, towards addressing any intelligence gaps they may have had in relation to him.

Of course, it would have been ideal if Ian Beggs had been placed on the sex offenders' register. If that had been the case, he would have been monitored more closely than he was, and his day-to-day whereabouts would probably have been known and recorded. But unfortunately, the crimes for which he had been prosecuted and convicted were not deemed to be of a sexual nature, and there was no requirement for his inclusion on the register.

As Geates and his team had been making preparations the previous evening for the planned search and arrest operation at Doon Place, Ian Beggs had been out partying at his work's Christmas dinner at the Forte Posthouse Hotel in Corstorphine. Around September that year, Beggs had applied for and been accepted in the post of a technical adviser working at Sykes call centre in Edinburgh. He was employed as part of a three-man team advising customers on technical issues relating to their Motorola mobile phones.

Rather than drink and drive, Beggs had partied with other Sykes employees until around 12.30am, and then had taken advantage of the special room rate his firm had negotiated with the hotel for those members of staff wanting to stay the night. Although he was fairly new to the company, Beggs immersed himself in the night's entertainment, dancing and laughing along with his new acquaintances. One particular colleague remembered him clearly that evening, as it had been commented that Beggs had a very distinctive laugh which could be heard a table or so away from where he was seated. From what he could remember, Beggs had seemed totally normal, and had spent a lot of the time at the bar talking to the other men at the event.

The next morning, Beggs was seen to appear for breakfast in the hotel restaurant, after which it was believed he made his way to the Sykes office for his normal shift. According to another employee who worked beside him, Beggs had been due to work nine to five that day, but as he arrived for his own shift that afternoon he noticed police seated at Beggs' computer terminal trawling through his e-mails. It seems that during the initial part of the search of Beggs' flat, the police had discovered documents, including payslips, which had led them to his place of work.

Sometime throughout the course of the day, possibly when surfing news channels on the computer, Ian Beggs had been alerted to the fact that police had carried out searches in the Bellfield area of Kilmarnock in relation to the Barry Wallace murder. As he had done in 1987 after the Barry Oldham murder, Beggs made the decision to run.

Throughout the early days of the hunt for Barry Wallace's murderer, the Scottish press seemed to be continually criticising the way the police were handling the investigation. With the spotlight well and truly on events at Doon Place, and a refusal by police to confirm they were looking for any suspects at that time, journalists sensed a bigger, more controversial story. Why – when they were already well aware of having such a violent offender living within the community who had a history of similar offences – did the police wait 12 days after the discovery of the limbs in the loch to move on Ian Beggs? Why also were they now refusing to name the suspect, even though it seemed everyone knew upon whom their efforts were concentrated?

On 20 December, the *Record* printed an in-depth story with the bold title 'WHY DID RIPPER GO FREE?' Alongside the scathing comments about the steps the police had taken up to that point in their enquiries, the newspaper printed a grainy photograph of Beggs and, beside that, a cherished family photograph of a young Barry Wallace smiling for the camera in bow tie and dress shirt. Under Scottish law, the newspapers are fully within their rights to publish a photograph of someone they believed to be involved in a crime, but only up until the point where a warrant is granted for an arrest. Thereafter, there would have been restrictions on any images of the suspect being printed in any publication. They were also at liberty to speculate on any aspects of the investigation and, throughout the article published on 20 December, they did much more than merely speculate. Intertwined with quotes from Detective Superintendent Geates, and a synopsis of the events from 6 December, the paper turned to Edinburgh-based psychologist Dr Ian Stephen for his particular take on the situation.

According to the *Record*, Dr Stephen had been the inspiration for the TV series *Cracker*, a crime drama which centred around a Scottish criminal profiler with an addictive personality who assisted the police in various difficult and disturbing murder cases. It is not clear the extent of Dr Stephen's willing participation in the article, but, with comments such as, 'If he [Beggs] is a serial killer, he will be under growing pressure and very tense. And one way for people like this to relieve tension is to carry out the act again,' fear and panic inevitably spread.

Although the flow of information was very limited, Dr Stephen speculated that the killer could well have been 'toying' with police, and may have deliberately placed the head on Barassie Beach. He also concurred with comments made by police that details of exactly what had happened to Barry Wallace would only be revealed when the torso was recovered.

In another article printed a few days later, Dr Stephen declared that, in his expert opinion, the police search for the torso was almost certainly in vain. He added that, if it had been dumped with the other body parts, it would have appeared not long after the others. The conclusion he had arrived at was that the torso was probably stored somewhere else, 'possibly in a refrigerator'. In a direct quote from the article, Dr Stephen stated, 'It could be hidden safely in a lock-up. The perpetrator of this bizarre crime probably had no plans to release the torso until he was ready, depending on what his game plan was.'

He concluded by labelling the killer as a 'classic psychopath' who, in his opinion, liked to play games with the police. The newspapers were determined to pad the story out. Ian Beggs had escaped arrest and was on the run, but, instead of alerting the public to possible places where he may have fled, their focus was directed towards pointing accusatory fingers at Strathclyde Police.

It must be said, though, that to those who mattered most, Ian Wallace, his wife Christine and remaining son Colin, there were no such signs of discontentment. On 23 December, despite the initial statement from police stating that they were 99 per cent sure that the limbs in the loch had not belonged to Barry, Ian Wallace told the newspapers, 'The police have been absolutely magnificent. I can't praise them enough.'

7
Fight or Flight

Regardless of how high profile the Wallace murder had become, there was still an issue of limited manpower and where best to direct resources considering the flight of the prime suspect. There would always be distractions, of course; avenues still had to be explored if only to close them off as dead ends. But as more and more evidence was being recovered from the flat at Bellfield, Detective Superintendent Geates was confident enough to apportion almost half of his officers to the task of discovering Beggs' hideaway.

From what they knew of the events after the murder of Barry Oldham, it had to be considered that his first instincts would have been to run to the safety of his parental home in Northern Ireland. Over the years, regardless of his criminal past, his mother and father, William and Winifred, had supported him without question, refusing to believe that their son had been guilty of any of the crimes of which he had been convicted. So Strathclyde Police did exactly what North Yorkshire Police had done 12 years earlier and requested the assistance of the Royal Ulster Constabulary. As well as highlighting the possibility that Beggs could already be in the Province, having had a head start of a few days, they decided to hedge their bets and asked the RUC to track any vehicles disembarking at their well-used ferry terminals, in the hope that it would flag up the little red Peugeot 205 with the Northern Ireland registration plate which detectives knew him to be driving.

In 1999, while the peace process was moving slowly towards what most would hope to be a successful endgame, the security forces in Northern Ireland, essentially the Army and the RUC, were still employing technology to aid them in gathering intelligence on possible paramilitary suspects. Sophisticated cameras were employed to recognise and record vehicle registrations as they passed static observation points, which could either be covert or overt depending on where they were deployed. One of the obvious locations for cameras such as these was at points of entry and exit to the country, including ferry terminals. Their effectiveness was increased, of course, when the actual registration being sought was typed into the computer with a flag raised as being of interest immediately upon recognition. There was, of course, no such option for screening foot passengers on the ferry other than through the details they were using to purchase a ticket.

For Beggs to do the obvious thing and bolt for home was unlikely, but it was still a possibility. According to an article in the *Record* newspaper published on 23 December, the services of the SAS had been called upon to assist in carrying out continual surveillance on the Beggs family's large, detached home in County Down, in case the suspect had used an alternative form of travel, and had tried to sneak into the house by whatever means. The paper also claimed to have an insider within the police force who was close to the investigation, and who could confirm that it had taken Strathclyde a full five days before they considered sending anyone across the Irish Sea to make enquiries first hand, and they had only arrived there on 22 December.

A reporter for the *Record*, Steve Smith, had made the journey himself a day or so before, and had called at the family home to try to get a comment from whoever would speak to him. While there, he said that he had witnessed a male fitting Beggs' description leave the house and get into a red Peugeot 205 similar to that which Beggs was known to drive, and then speed off. The male had refused to answer any questions put to him by Smith, and had pulled the hood of his anorak tightly around his head, disguising his identity. When Smith reported on the encounter, homing in on the fact that the male had been similar in description to that of Ian Beggs, the police could do little but follow up. The male in question was never identified, but may have been one of Beggs' siblings or a relative.

As it transpired, Ian Beggs had ruled out going back to Northern Ireland, and in the short time after discovering he was being sought by police had used his knowledge of travel in and around Europe to plan a less obvious escape.

One has to remember that effectively Beggs had been caught on the hop. It was a Friday afternoon; he had what clothes he had taken for the work party the night before and whatever he had worn to work that day, assuming he had bothered to take a change of clothing with him. But, more importantly, he had very little money (although it would later become clear that he did have a cheque book and cheque card) and no passport. For someone less calculating, the options would have been limited. But for Beggs, a clever and resourceful individual, there were many ways to put distance between himself and police.

First, he drove overnight to Luton and left his car at the airport on the Saturday morning. This was the first red herring which he intended police to follow up on and to waste valuable time and effort. While at Luton, he cashed a cheque and bought French francs, an indication perhaps of his eventual destination. With notes in his pocket, though, he had the opportunity to change the francs for any other European currency at a bureau de change without leaving any trace of the transaction.

Instead of booking on to any flight at Luton, Beggs then

took public transport into London where he bought a ticket for a British Airways fight for the next day, Sunday, bound for Jersey out of Heathrow. He purchased the ticket in the name of William Frederick.

In the post-9/11 era, we are all too familiar with the restrictions of air travel, regardless of whether the journeys we take are domestic or international. Security at airports has tightened up beyond recognition, with passports and documentation only part and parcel of what we expect when travelling anywhere in the world. Back in 1999, however, it was possible to purchase a ticket with cash and jump on a plane, particularly internal flights within the UK, without so much as a driving licence or a sideways glance. The age of international terrorism has, if nothing else, made it much more difficult to travel freely by air and sea, and provides less options for fugitive suspects.

If the authorities had already alerted the airport and ferry portals to the possibility that Ian Beggs could be making his way to mainland Europe, they must not have considered the Channel Islands, or the fact that he may have been travelling under an alias. His flight to Jersey went without incident and, on arrival, he was able to purchase a flight to Dinard near St Malo in France, again without the use of a passport. From there it is believed he went to Paris by train, and eventually on to Amsterdam, probably by the same means.

After his initial purchase of francs at Luton, Beggs had desisted from using any method other than cash to make a transaction. Even though he had managed to get to the Netherlands undetected, Beggs must have known that, without money and without official papers, he could only run for so long before he would either be caught or would have to hand himself in. What he had really achieved was to slow the whole process down, to delay the inevitable and to give himself an opportunity to plan his next move.

On 28 December, Ian Beggs walked into the Vreemdelingen (foreigners) police station in Amsterdam with his Dutch lawyer, Lian Mannheims, and told the desk sergeant on duty, 'I'm wanted by the Scottish police. I'm here to give myself up.'

Within minutes, checks were made with Interpol and Strathclyde and, after confirmation, Beggs was arrested and taken into custody. According to Klaus Wilting, a spokesman for the Dutch police, in the hours after his arrest, Beggs had spoken very little, other than to voice his fears at being returned to a Scottish prison. He was being coached very carefully by Lian Mannheims, who insisted her client would be rigorously denying any allegations being made by police in Scotland, and that she would be fighting any attempts to extradite Beggs from Holland. If there were any enquiries to be made with her client regarding a murder in Scotland, she wanted those enquiries to be made while he was in custody in Bijlmerbajes Penitentiary on Dutch soil.

Although Beggs was now in custody as such, frustratingly the detectives in Scotland were possibly even further away from having the opportunity to put questions to him. Before anything else could be done, an application for extradition had to be made in the appropriate manner for processing in the Dutch courts. First of all, formal charges had to be drawn up at the Kilmarnock Sheriff Court, and then, armed with the petition for extradition, one of the Wallace investigation team, accompanied by an official from the Scottish Crown Office, would travel to Holland where they would give those instructions to a Dutch Crown lawyer. In turn, they would place the request before the Dutch court for consideration.

Primarily for the order to be granted, the offences of which the proposed extraditee was accused had to be criminal offences in both countries, which, if convicted, carried a custodial sentence of more than one year. In respect of this, there would be no difficulty at all, as Beggs was alleged to have committed murder and abduction. But more importantly, and crucial to the application, was that the judge presiding over the petition had to be satisfied that the applicants had provided enough evidence against the party in custody to support a trial before they leaned towards granting extradition to another jurisdiction.

As the Netherlands is a member of the European Union, it was unlikely that there would be any diplomatic or political issues to stymie the proceedings. Regardless of that fact, though, the whole process, from a formal request for extradition being lodged by Strathclyde Police, until the Dutch court's decision and any possible appeal against an unfavourable outcome for Beggs, could take as long as six months to a year. There was simply no way to hurry things up.

Extradition cases in general were not that common, but there had been a relatively high-profile case involving a British criminal who had been linked to money laundering from the notorious Brinks Mat robbery in 1983. In 1996, Kenneth (Kenny) Noye, a well-known underworld figure, was being sought in connection with the brutal stabbing to death of motorist Stephen Cameron on the M25. Police investigating the case were made aware of his presence in Spain some two years later, but had to wait until March 1999, a period of eight months from his initial arrest outside a Spanish restaurant in August 1998, before they were finally able to return him for trial in England.

Using Noyes' example as a benchmark, Detective Superintendent Geates prepared to dig in for the long wait. It was a bitter pill for the Scottish authorities to swallow; they were confident of Beggs' guilt in the Wallace murder, but weren't able immediately to lay hands on him. The only positive thing they could take from the situation was that they could now concentrate on the job of building a solid case against him, content that, for now at least, he was not at large. When the decision to grant them extradition of their suspect would arrive — and in their minds it was when and not if — they would have a case-ready file with which to take him before the court.

The differences between the laws in Scotland and that of the rest of mainland Britain and Northern Ireland are many. In cases of criminal law in Scotland, a potential suspect can be detained by police in order to assist them with their enquiries. The maximum they can detain a suspect for is six hours, and the clock counting down those six hours starts immediately upon detention, wherever that may be. Within that time, after administering a caution, the police may question the suspect, usually during a tape-recorded interview. Once that time has elapsed, however, the police must either release the suspect or formally arrest and charge them.

There are no second bites of the cherry as such; once someone has been detained for a six-hour period for an offence, it cannot be repeated. Those of us who are not acquainted with the workings of Scottish legal procedure could be forgiven for thinking that the scales are tipped well and truly in favour of the suspect. However, the one aspect of the detention period which the police can use to their advantage is the fact that the detainee is not entitled to the presence of a solicitor, although it has to be said that some Scottish constabularies will, on occasion, let the suspect consult with their legal representatives during that period.

Once the detention period is exhausted and a decision is made to charge the suspect, then there can be no more questions put to them. It is then the responsibility of the police to have the suspect before the next available court, more often than not the next day, otherwise any further detention is deemed illegal.

Responsibility for investigating any crime in Scotland lies well and truly with the police, although on completion of any such investigation it is the Procurator Fiscal and the Crown Office who make the decision to prosecute the matter. There is no second guessing in matters of serious crime such as murder or rape, for instance. The Procurator Fiscal will, on consideration of the evidence presented to them by police, direct on matters such as any planned detention and arrest. The police will then further the investigation through questioning and hopefully attain further evidence with which to secure a prosecution at the High Court.

In contrast, in the rest of the UK, forgoing minor differences between England, Wales and Northern Ireland, a person suspected of a fairly serious offence is usually subject to arrest, which then, and only then, provides the police with the opportunity to obtain further evidence of that offence through questioning. The form of the questioning is a tape-recorded interview or interviews, which will be carried out at a custody suite in a police station. All aspects of police procedure are laid out in PACE (Police and Criminal Evidence Act 1984), and this also dictates the amount of time a suspect can be detained for, that being 24 hours, or 36 hours if a superintendent has authorised further detention, having been satisfied that it is necessary to 'preserve evidence relating to an offence' or 'obtain such evidence by questioning'. The offence has to be an indictable offence, and the superintendent has to agree that the investigation is being conducted 'diligently' and 'expeditiously'. The detention period starts as soon as the person crosses the threshold of the police station, and is referred to as the 'relevant time'. In other words, as soon as a suspect is brought into the confines of a police station, their detention begins, and their PACE clock begins to tick.

In cases where there are exhibits, the investigating officers will want to be able to show those exhibits to the suspect and ask them to account for them. If those exhibits are not readily available at the time of the first interviews, or as in other cases have to be submitted for DNA or fingerprint comparisons, then the police will have the option to release the suspect on bail to return at a later date when that evidence can be put to them for explanation.

Evidence can be outstanding for all sorts of reasons, as in a drugs case perhaps, where substances have had to be submitted for forensic analysis, or simple shoplifting where CCTV images have to be downloaded and processed. Whatever the offence, and regardless of how insignificant the outstanding evidence may be, the suspect is always afforded the right to be shown that evidence and given the opportunity to provide an explanation for, or deny any involvement with, the items they are being shown.

Like their Scottish counterparts, if the police are satisfied with the strength of their evidence against a suspect, they will normally charge that person to appear at court. It can be an overnight charge for some serious offences or for a habitual repeat offender, who may pose a threat to someone else or themselves for that matter, but as is more often the case the suspect is charged to appear at court any time within a 28-day period.

If the offence is of a nature where the investigating officer has no concerns with releasing the suspect, and is sure that they will turn up for court if summonsed, then they can be released from custody pending the outcome of a report compiled for the Public Prosecution Service.

In a murder case, where the available evidence is overwhelming, it would be extremely unlikely that, after the interview process had been exhausted, the suspect would not be charged overnight to appear in court the next day with a strong recommendation for a remand in custody until trial.

There is no doubt there are clear differences in procedure, but it doesn't necessarily mean that the suspect is advantaged in any way. The law in Scotland has always protected an individual's right to liberty at all costs, a concept reinforced by the Human Rights Act 1998. Any decision to interfere with a person's liberty is only taken if absolutely necessary, so one can fully understand why the Procurator Fiscal will only issue a warrant of arrest when satisfied there is no other alternative.

When Ian Beggs eventually handed himself in to police in Amsterdam, the criticism which the press had aimed at Strathclyde Police seemed to dissipate. There was no longer a threat to the community at large. The prime suspect was in custody, regardless of what country that was in, and their focus now turned towards the extradition plans and the progress police were making in uncovering the details of the secret life of Ian Beggs, the serial killer.

8

Inside the Mind of a Killer

When Ian Beggs became the prime suspect in the Barry Wallace murder and his photograph was plastered across the newspapers, the team who had worked on the Barry Oldham murder back in 1987 were reminded of just how close they had come to frustrating Beggs' criminal career. Head of North Yorkshire CID at the time, Tony Fitzgerald, had been extremely vocal about Beggs' release in 1989: 'When we caught Beggs all those years ago, we seriously thought we had caught a serial killer in the making.' He went on to say, 'We thought we were lucky because we had managed to catch him after his first killing.'

It stands to reason that there would have been a degree of bitterness in reaction to the successful outcome of Beggs' appeal in 1989, among both friends and family of Oldham and the police inquiry team themselves. The sadistic nature of the murder had always suggested to the police that Beggs had done something similar before and would be capable of doing so again. Now they were certain. William Ian Frederick Beggs was a serial killer.

But was it correct to regard Beggs as a bona fide serial killer, and what criteria have to be applied before someone is considered to be a serial killer? And who actually decided upon those criteria in the first place? It appears that the term was first used in the 1980s when the FBI in the United States applied it to describe killers who seemed to be choosing their victims from particular groups, killing again and again and using a signature modus operandi. Each of their murders was a continuance in a series, hence the term 'serial'.

The film and television industries, along with the increasingly popular crime-fiction genre, can be blamed for popularising the term, with novels, movies and TV shows taking the serial killer theme to the next level and chilling audiences with ever more depraved storylines.

As far as the FBI was concerned, though, the rule of thumb when considering whether they were hunting a serial killer was if they had committed at least three separate murders, at different locations, and with a time period of days, weeks or often longer separating each crime. There were other people responsible for multiple homicides, of course, but these were categorised as either mass murders – those who killed four or more victims all at the same time in the same place, such as the single episodes of mass murder at Columbine or Dunblane – or spree killings, those who carried out murders at two or more locations without a cooling-off period in between.

With a label now generally agreed upon, the term 'serial killer' could be applied retrospectively to already infamous characters such as Jack the Ripper and Albert De Salvo, known as the Boston Strangler. When the term is wheeled out during an investigation into multiple homicides, it strikes fear and panic into the very heart of the community.

Over the years, there have been countless articles and books written about some of the world's most notorious serial killers, and I am sure that most of us will be able to recount one fact or another about some of the better known. I myself would never profess to being an expert on any particular one, but there is one story which I did recall quite vividly as I was writing this book. After rooting through the various hardbacks I had stored away, I was able to refresh my memory. It was the similarity with the circumstances surrounding Brian McQuillan's attack back in July 1991 which had made me flick through the chapters until I reached the one dedicated to Jeffrey Dahmer.

Coincidentally, on 27 May of that same year, 1991, thousands of miles away in a neglected neighbourhood of Milwaukee in the USA, two young black women contacted the local police after finding a naked teenage boy of Asian extraction wandering the streets. They thought the boy was in his mid to late teens, but couldn't get any details from him as he wasn't making much sense, as if he were drunk or on drugs.

By the time a patrol car arrived with three police officers on board, a tall, blond-haired male had joined the two women and was arguing with them and trying to coax the young man to come away with him. One of the officers spoke to the male, who explained that the young Asian man was, in fact, 19 years of age, and his boyfriend. According to him, they had had a row, and the young man had become drunk and wandered off. He then showed the officer his ID in the name of Jeffrey Dahmer, and pointed out the apartment block he lived in a short distance away. The two young women were far from happy and tried to explain that, as they had stood waiting for police to arrive, Dahmer had been trying to drag the young man away against his will.

Despite how much the two women protested, the police accepted Dahmer's story and escorted both males back to his apartment. The young Asian man was then sat down on the sofa in the living room to recover, and the police officers made the decision to leave what they believed to be the gay couple alone with their domestic dispute. They had noticed a strange smell when inside the apartment, but hadn't thought to investigate at the time. Had they been tempted to probe further, they would have found that the smell was emanating from a decomposing body in the bedroom. A 31-

year-old man, Tony Hughes, had been murdered there only three days before, and Dahmer had not got around to disposing of his body.

Some weeks later, when the press released photographs of a missing person – a young male originally from Laos by the name of Konerak Simthasomphone – the two women who had stood on the street with the naked teenager that May agreed that it was the same person. Again, they contacted police and urged them to look into the incident, but the information wasn't acted upon.

Just a matter of a few months later, police patrolling the same area in Milwaukee came across a young man wandering the streets with handcuffs attached to one of his wrists. Suspecting he may have escaped from another patrol in the area, they detained him. Although he was a little confused, Tracy Edwards was clear that he had just come from the apartment of what he described as a 'weird dude' who had just drugged him and tried to kill him with a knife.

The police then took the man back to the apartment at 924 North 25th Street, and the door was opened by Jeffrey Dahmer. Again, though, this unremarkable-looking white man apologised for wasting police time, and said that he would retrieve the handcuff key from his bedroom to set the young man free. As he moved towards the bedroom, Edwards reminded the officers that the knife Dahmer had used on him was probably still in the bedroom and one of the officers decided to search the room himself. What the police officer saw in the room were several photographs of what appeared to be body parts: limbs and severed heads.

The officer called out to his partner and, after a brief struggle, Dahmer was arrested and handcuffed. When one of the officers opened up the fridge door, he was dumbfounded to find a severed head staring back at him. A detailed search of the apartment revealed the decomposing bodies of four other men in an acid bath, and a selection of human body parts in various cooking pots. There were also three severed heads and a human heart in the freezer. When Dahmer was questioned, he claimed to have murdered a total of 17 men over a prolonged period.

The young Asian man, Konerak Simthasomphone, who had managed to escape naked from Dahmer's apartment earlier that year only to be led straight back there, was among the body count. He was 14 years old. During interviews, Dahmer admitted that after police had left the apartment that night he had strangled and killed the boy and then had sex with his corpse. He then told police that he had dismembered the body, and, although he had intended to dispose of the limbs, he had kept the head as a souvenir, boiling it up in a pot to remove the flesh from it, and then stored it in his fridge.

Like Brian McQuillan, Tracy Edwards had found enough inner strength to kick and punch his way past a man who was hell bent on murdering him and, like McQuillan, the actions he took undoubtedly saved his life. For 14-year-old

Simthasomphone, however, the outcome was tragic. Having come so close to finding asylum from this monster, Konerak was to be let down by the very people he would have expected he could count on, the Milwaukee Police Department.

There were numerous repercussions following the revelation that the police had delivered this young man back into the hands of a killer, even more when it was suggested that they had clearly taken the word of a white man over that of two black women. Racial tension was always bubbling away below the surface in Milwaukee, but tempers frayed further and people took to the streets. There was also the issue of homophobic comments made by the attending officers to their dispatcher on that night in May, which forced the hand of the police department into dismissing two of them, only to reinstate them later after an appeal.

There has been more than one occasion when the press have made comparisons between Beggs and Dahmer. In terms of depravity, Dahmer's murders rate among the worst ever recorded, but others, like those carried out by John Wayne Gacy and Dennis Nilsen, two other names mentioned in articles alongside Ian Beggs, must run them close for that dubious honour.

Notorious killer John Wayne Gacy, executed in the United States in May 1994 for no less than 33 murders, had been able to evade detection by projecting the image of a hard-working, generous and affable businessman with all the trappings of success. In reality, Gacy was a violent, homosexual paedophile who would cruise the streets of Chicago preying on young runaway or homeless boys, whom he would take back to his house, torture, rape and then strangle.

As a child, Gacy had had to contend with a violent, alcoholic father who had regarded his son as effeminate, and had physically abused him. It seemed the young Gacy always found it difficult coming to terms with his sexuality; his conviction and brief incarceration for minor sexual assaults on boys caused the breakdown of his first marriage. His second wife soon also found that Gacy preferred young boys and men, and she moved out, too, not knowing that the murders had already begun. Most of Gacy's victims were found by police search teams in the crawl space under his house.

A former army cook and police recruit, Nilsen eventually aimed for anonymity working within the civil service in a job centre in London. He had already had his first homosexual experience before leaving the Army, but there had never been any long-term relationships in his life, and he described himself as a lonely individual.

He would kill for the first time in December 1978, strangling a young man he had just met that evening in a pub. He had taken the boy home to his little flat in Cricklewood, where they had sex and then, fearing the young man would not stay with him, Nilsen killed him. He then washed the body down and secreted it under the floorboards. It would be

August the next year before he eventually parted with the boy's remains by dismembering the body and burning the limbs on a fire in the garden. Up until then, he had taken the body from its hiding place on more than one occasion to keep him company. He would repeat this behaviour with the corpse of another of his victims, Kenneth Ockenden, removing him from his hiding place under the floor and propping him up beside him in bed or on the sofa when he watched television.

When he moved flats to Muswell Hill in London, Nilsen found he had nowhere to hide the bodies he was accumulating and took to cutting them up and flushing them down the toilet. With particularly awkward body parts such as the head, he would first boil them up in a pot to help remove the flesh and then flush them as before. In all, Nilsen would admit to 15 murders; all were males and some would never be identified.

Serial killers share many similarities, and it was exactly that realisation which led the FBI to begin assimilating information and using it to help create a profile of offenders as their crimes came to light. The use of profiling can be traced back as far as the 1950s when Howard Teten and Pat Mullany, two FBI employees, were instrumental in creating a research and development department solely concentrating on criminal profiling in the form of the Behavioural Science Unit.

Over a number of years, a mass of data was accumulated

through extensive interviews with violent criminals, including convicted serial killers. From family background, sexual orientation and psychological traits, each aspect was recorded and then compared against similar types of offenders. Poring over details of crime scenes and identifying a killer's signature and modus operandi are all part and parcel of piecing together a profile which can then be presented to the detectives in charge of an investigation.

It has to be said, though, that profiling is no substitute for solid police work and tried and tested investigative techniques. What it can do, however, is assist the investigator to narrow down any list of suspects, thereby directing resources to where they would prove most effective.

If used, the FBI's profiling technique is divided into five stages. The first stage is the gathering and inputting of any relevant information attained about a crime, which could include witness accounts, victim profile, any physical evidence and post-mortem findings. Next, the profiler will organise the material inputted so that pertinent questions relating to the type of criminal activity involved can be posed. For instance, what was the primary motive for the attack (such as sexual or personal)? Where did the crime take place, and was the body moved from the original crime scene? Third, from the findings of the previous two stages, the profiler attempts to reconstruct the behaviour of both the killer and the victim. The killer will either have been organised or impulsive, or by virtue of the injuries caused during the attack will have identified themselves as having known the victim or at least lived in close proximity.

The next stage will involve producing a working profile for the investigator including type of employment, age range, marital status, beliefs and moral values and the possibility that there has been an offending history. Last and most important, that profile is taken by an investigator and compared against any possible suspects they may have already identified. This is very much a synopsis of the process, of course. Compiling a working profile during an active investigation is much more involved, often with reams and reams of data being collected and applied to the system.

To try and determine whether Ian Beggs really does share traits with other serial killers, it is useful to make comparisons. Like Dahmer, Gacy and Nilsen, Beggs was a violent homosexual who preyed on men with whom he had no previous relationship. Each of these killers would incapacitate their victims in one way or another, sexually assault them whether they were dead or alive, and then dispose of the bodies.

These may all appear to be superficial similarities, coincidences perhaps, but it has been determined that killers do have identifiable patterns. Their crimes are about domination and control, but there is almost always a sexual motivation, even though the crime scene may not always indicate this. The killing itself is both emotionally fulfilling and empowering for the murderer, more so as they move successfully from one victim to the next. By evading detection, they develop a feeling of superiority, which has the effect of further empowering them.

Regardless of how well adjusted and successful they may have appeared in the real world, most serial killers will have harboured feelings of underachievement and inferiority. The crimes they commit have given them control, both over their own lives and that of others, in particular, of course, their victims.

As the murders are uncovered and an investigation begins, the serial killer will follow any developments closely, maybe to the extent of keeping a scrap book on press releases or making notes in a diary or journal. There is a possibility that the killer will also have taken a memento or 'trophy' at the time of the crime, a lock of hair perhaps, a piece of clothing or jewellery, or even a body part. These 'trophies' will help them relive the event and sustain the killer through a lean period when they have had to refrain from killing for one reason or another.

There are no rules or guidelines as to how long a serial killer will continue to offend. Often they stop themselves when they realise that killing no longer fulfils them in any way, or they may take their own lives. But many feel compelled to continue until they are either caught or come to a natural end themselves.

There has always been a train of thought that killers do what they do because basically they are evil people. It is a very simplistic explanation, but not terribly helpful if we intend to apply science to try to identify potentially high-risk individuals who are both capable of and likely to kill without thought of consequence.

In his 2002 book *Base Instincts: What Makes Killers Kill*, neurologist Jonathan Pincus concludes that most violent criminals are the product of an abusive family upbringing coupled with brain damage and possibly mental illness. Over a period of 25 years, he personally examined over 100 murderers, some of whom were on death row awaiting their fate. He also probed extensively into their family backgrounds and relationships, often uncovering the most horrific physical, mental and sexual abuse and, in some cases, identifying a singular incident where the individual received acute injuries to the head causing severe trauma to the frontal lobes of the brain.

His views are shared by many. According to Dr Phillip S Hicks, former Chief Psychiatrist at San Quentin Prison in California, the relevance of brain disease is 'vastly under-diagnosed'. The result of determining the extent of brain damage found in some of the killers Pincus examined was that some were spared execution, with their sentences commuted to life imprisonment. There was no 'get out of jail free card', and no reason or grounds to retry any cases based on the defendants' unfortunate circumstances. They had committed the crimes they had been imprisoned for; the evidence in some cases was considerable and way beyond doubt. But perhaps if we were to examine the details of their own misfortune, then we could at least begin to understand just why they acted in the way they did.

It is generally agreed in law-enforcement circles in the United States that there are certain early indicators that precede violent and antisocial tendencies, such as enuresis (bed wetting) which takes place at an inappropriate age, cruelty to animals or small children, and instances of arson whether on a large or small scale. This triad of behavioural indicators is by no means definitive, but, should a potential suspect be identified as having experienced episodes of all three, the emphasis of an investigation will shift towards them and they will quickly become a prime suspect.

I am convinced that Beggs fits into the category of a serial killer, regardless of the fact that to date there has only been enough evidence to link and convict him of the murder of two victims. These techniques were never really applied to either murder case, but if they had been he would certainly have ticked several of the positive indicators. As it was, there was never any need to request a profile in the Barry Oldham murder back in 1987, as police were confident the answer had lain within the gay community, particularly those people who had attended Rockshots on the night Oldham was killed. They also had a solid sighting of a man and a distinctive vehicle at the body dump site which proved to be invaluable. And, when Barry Wallace was found butchered 12 years later, the police already had a suspect in mind and, as we've discovered already from a police 'insider', Beggs was well known to officers on the force.

With regard to issues in his formative years which may have shaped his potential for offending, there may be clues in the conversations he would have with friend and confidante Richard Bache. They appear in the form of tales which Beggs recounts to Bache, citing other people, mutual friends or acquaintances, as the victims of physical or sexual abuse during childhood. The circumstances of this abuse, which Beggs describes in respect of the family members involved, are in Richard Bache's opinion strikingly similar to what he knows of the domestic make-up of the Beggs family back in Northern Ireland. He is clear that Beggs never at any point said that he had been abused, but he saw clear parallels in the stories, and even suggested that Beggs may have been projecting these experiences on to other people.

Without the co-operation of Beggs in relation to an exploration of his childhood and potential triggers for his violent and sociopathic behaviour, it will remain speculation. What is clear, though, is the fact that Beggs' sexuality has always been in question and, when looked at against a faith-based upbringing, may very well be the catalyst which turned him into a killer.

From what we know of the young Ian Beggs and his years spent in the company of other developing teenagers and the period beyond, we can detect a pattern of behaviour which suggests that of a gay or homosexual man raging against what he has been taught to believe are base and unnatural desires. His attempts to suppress these feelings lead him towards extreme displays of heterosexual behaviour, as in his joining the 'Save Ulster from Sodomy' campaign, and adopting the image of a long-haired, heavy-metal biker, an exaggerated stereotyping of the red-blooded macho male. These can be interpreted as clear reactions to homophobia (often explained as an individual's fear or hatred of all things related to homosexuality), and a desperation to prove to himself – but, more importantly, to others around him – that he is a straight man.

As for the rest of his life, Beggs continually presented himself as a leader not a follower, and this assertiveness may have again helped to mask an inferiority complex which could have developed during his school years. In most cases, adolescent straight males and females develop feelings of superiority towards homosexuals. Their development from spotty youths into young men and women has been less fraught, in contrast to that of a homosexual, as there is no stigma attached to being heterosexual. Consequently, they appear more well-adjusted individuals with good social skills, a strong sense of self-identity and higher self-esteem. Homosexuals are faced with the difficulties of dealing with prejudice as being part of a stigmatised group, which can in turn make them susceptible to mental-health episodes, depression and substance abuse. In the extreme, it can lead to suicide.

When an adolescent struggling with their sexuality at school witnesses their male peers' testosterone-fuelled attempts at impressing the class pin-up, or alternately a girl revelling in the power of her female allure over anxious, sweating, teenage boys, they will quickly recognise the acceptable face of sexuality in a fiercely competitive and potentially hostile environment. Faced with the possible consequences of ridicule, bullying and ostracism for the duration of their remaining school days, who would then want to present themselves as anything other than a heterosexual male or female? Faking it may seem like the easy option, but leading what effectively is a double life can have negative consequences on one's emotional and psychological wellbeing.

In many instances, in an attempt to prove they are straight, some individuals (both heterosexual and homosexual) use sex itself to try to rubber stamp their sexual identity. They can become so promiscuous in their sexual relationships that STDs and teenage pregnancies are prevalent, and it has been suggested that there are links between this extreme heterosexual behaviour and sexual abuse or even rape. This need to affirm one's sexuality as that of a heterosexual male, or for that matter as a female, can be destructive, but only if one allows it be.

Ian Beggs was, I believe, a homosexual man in total denial, continually craving his parents' approval, but particularly his mother's, knowing full well that his parents' faith denounced homosexuality as an abomination. This – coupled with feelings of superiority driven by his keen intellect – only succeeded in compounding the guilt he may have felt at seeking the company of gay men, a trait he would have considered a weakness. He may have tried to convince himself that it was they (the gay men he picked up and brought home) who had exerted some seductive influence over him, forcing him into physical, homosexual liaisons in which he had not been a willing party. Angry and ashamed, and feeling that he had been taken advantage of, he then meted out his own brand of punishment, which in some way absolved him of his involvement in the liaison. He becomes the 'alpha male' figure, subduing his prey, and cutting and slicing at will.

It could also explain why he moved towards singling out heterosexual males in the days after the attack on Brian McQuillan, when he cruised the streets of Glasgow and further afield looking for victims. Having chosen to surrender to a life centred around the gay community, but only ever admitting to having an 'eclectic' sex life, he may have wanted to punish and humiliate those people he was deeply jealous of – the straight males with no sexual hang-ups; the very type of person he believed would ridicule gays or 'limp-wristed queers'. Who better to blame for his inner torment than those confident, self-assured, straight men? In some ways, it may also have been about the challenge, in that, although the sex would never have been consensual, he may have believed his victims could have been aroused during the act, proof in his mind that, like him, they had no control over their sexual desires.

This is all conjecture on my part, of course, and Ian Beggs himself may not even be able to provide a rationale for his own decision-making process. Each episode may be the result of involuntary actions carried out in a state of sexual euphoria. But everything else he does before and after these acts is controlled and measured.

Interestingly, though, as with many serial killers for whom the aspect of control within their lives is paramount, in the last few weeks before the Wallace murder, Richard Bache believes that Beggs was showing signs of stress. From what he remembered, Beggs had exhausted any monies set aside for his PhD, and had made very little progress, spending less and less time on his studies and more time at work. How better then to regain control in his life than to control someone else's? The fact that the product of that control would or could mean someone losing their life meant absolutely nothing to Ian Beggs.

For that reason alone, he is undoubtedly one of the most dangerous men walking the landings of Peterhead Jail. A man without conscience, and a natural born killer.

9

With Friends Like These...

In the days immediately after the raid on Beggs' flat and his disappearance, police began the painstaking process of sifting through documents and items seized at Doon Place in an attempt to learn more about the person they were hunting. At that time, they had no idea that Beggs would hand himself in a week or so later and, locked into a murder investigation and a manhunt, clues to his whereabouts could very well have been among the countless papers and files taken from the little flat. What they were also hoping to achieve, though, was to build up a picture of their suspect, his lifestyle, routines and, more importantly, any close friends or acquaintances he may have had.

Even at this stage of the investigation, it was apparent to all that such was the violence and cruelty of Barry's murder that there was the very real possibility that Beggs had struck before, and that they could come across evidence relating to other crimes and more victims. In light of Beggs' well-documented criminal past, it was hard to imagine that he would have waited nearly five years after his release from prison for his attack on Brian McQuillan to strike again. What had he done in the interim period?

It may have seemed like an impossible task even to consider trying to establish anything about Beggs' movements over a longer time period than the days and weeks surrounding the murder of Wallace. There may have been the odd credit-card receipt or bank statement which could prove withdrawals or purchases at certain times in certain places, but they would need much more than that. And much more they would get!

What they didn't expect was a person to step forward voluntarily, identifying himself as someone who knew Beggs on a friendship basis, and admitting to spending a great deal of time with the man over a period from the end of 1995 through to the weekend of 4–5 December 1999, the very day that Barry Wallace disappeared.

You only have to spend a matter of minutes in the company of Richard Bache to appreciate the negative impact Ian Beggs has had on his life. Although he was never harmed physically by the man he knew and described as being a 'mate' and a 'good friend', his mental health has undoubtedly suffered and, in turn, certain aspects of his career and private life have also been affected.

The strange reality of being Richard Bache is that, despite the fact that the assistance he gave to police during their investigation was substantial – so much so that he would prove to be a key witness for the prosecution during the subsequent trial – he would still be treated by some colleagues and students alike with a degree of suspicion because of his association with Beggs.

To be able to understand how and why Bache was left traumatised after learning about the murder of Barry Wallace and the fact that his friend Ian Beggs was responsible, you have to first comprehend the relationship between the two men. I spoke at length to Richard Bache at his spartan but relatively spacious flat on the outskirts of Glasgow. He appeared slightly nervous at first, but totally rational and rather determined. Like Brian McQuillan, over time he had gathered together numerous newspaper clippings and articles relating to the investigation and the trial, along with printed copies of e-mails sent between Beggs and himself during the period from July to the end of October 1999, as well as copies of the notes he first made for police prior to making a full statement.

It wasn't the first time Bache had spoken of his involvement with Beggs. He had already been involved in the making of a short television documentary about the murder and the man who had become known as 'the gay ripper', although he had insisted on protecting his identity by asking them to film only his profile from behind during the interview. As with any production for television, time is limited, and perhaps it was difficult for Bache to convey his message completely. If nothing else, the written word could help others to realise the difficulties he had faced after being identified as Beggs' closest friend while being a totally innocent party, as oblivious to the machinations of Beggs' evil mind as any of the people who had either worked alongside Bache or been one of his students.

The man he knew was articulate and incredibly engaging, slotting easily into any social surroundings, regardless of how daunting they may have seemed to others. Even though it was Bache who was the lecturer and Beggs who was the student, it was Beggs who was able to draw on his huge list of contacts to gain invites to parties, lectures or formal evenings. In his opinion, there was always an air of confidence about Beggs, and a sense of humour which Bache first describes as 'wicked', and then, after pausing, decides to revise as being 'sick'.

I trust Richard Bache would agree that since that Christmas in 1999 he has had time to dissect every aspect of Beggs' behaviour, as much as his recollections will let him. There may be a trace of paranoia in his interpretations of conversations, trips or events, and their significance in relation to the investigation of the Barry Wallace murder and after, but who could blame him?

For close to three years, the two men had an ordinary relationship as friends, whereby they discussed every topic under the sun from their religious beliefs to their taste in music. As Richard Bache had told me when I first contacted him, in those three years, had someone told him that his friend Ian Beggs hadn't paid his television licence, he would have been astounded.

It was 1990 when Richard Bache, a research fellow at Glasgow Caledonian College (now Glasgow University), first met the young Ulsterman. He recalled that at the time Beggs had been employed as a housing officer and they moved in similar circles in the gay scene. Back then, he knew him only as Ian; no surnames were either sought or necessary, and their conversations were usually about the PhD Bache had been studying for. Coincidentally, Bache was also friendly with Brian McQuillan but, as it transpired, neither man would ever be aware of that connection until after the Barry Wallace murder.

In the three or four years after that first encounter, Richard Bache was to leave Glasgow and return to London, his city of birth, where he worked for the City of London. He was restless, though, and, despite how good the money was, he chose to move back and forwards between the two cities. London had its attractions, of course, but Bache found he was more in tune with the people and the landscape in Glasgow, and he eventually settled there at the beginning of 1996, having secured a job at Paisley University.

Prior to that application, just four weeks earlier, at New Year celebrations in the city, Bache had bumped into his old acquaintance Ian at a pub called the Waterloo. When Bache told Beggs about his forthcoming interview for the vacant post in the department covering computing, Beggs explained that he was a student at Paisley completing his Master's in the very same subject and they agreed to meet up on the day. It was indeed a coincidence, but there was something else happening between the two men which appeared to be drawing them together. It wasn't a sexual attraction as such, rather a meeting of minds; two similar-aged men, both of whom could be described as academics, and neither into small-talk for the sake of prolonging conversation.

The friendship eventually developed into one of mutual benefit. Both men were not native to Scotland, and they enjoyed taking off for trips to everywhere and anywhere around the country at a whim. It was Beggs who had the car and could drive, and seemed to know the geography of Scotland better than Bache did, often pointing out interesting sites or attractions as they went to one destination or another.

In the department Bache worked in, they would often shoot videos to assist the students with their course development and, as with any small productions, they were forever seeking out locations and approaching people for permission to film on their property. The fact that Beggs had a car and was willing to get involved was a plus, of course, and he soon became a key participant in the whole project.

These little jaunts they took soon developed a pattern of

their own. As Beggs still lived in Kilmarnock and Bache in Glasgow, he would invariably telephone Bache first before he drove from one place to the other. And, when out on one of their trips, they would almost always stop for a meal somewhere, and it was Bache who would always pay with a credit or debit card. To even the monies out for the day's expenses, Beggs would deduct an amount for the petrol used, and give Bache whatever was owed in cash. It may sound like a moot point, but, when questioned later by police, Bache would be able to look through his credit-card statements and be able to determine where and on what dates he had been with Beggs and exactly what they had been doing on that day, and for what reason, if any.

Beggs had certain traits that Richard Bache would become accustomed to over time, his stubbornness being the obvious one. If Beggs had set his mind to doing something, then there would be little that could distract him from his goal. He applied this single-minded approach to everything he did, but particularly in respect of the obsession he had with the law, and the various legal actions he undertook. Bache recalled that on one occasion Beggs had his car towed away by police because of a parking violation. He seemed absolutely livid and immediately challenged the issue by choosing to go to court. After inspecting the signage and road markings where he had parked, and on reading about the road traffic restrictions and implications, he represented himself on the day, stating a point of law, and won his case.

There were also occasions when he took up grievances on behalf of other members of his family; actions were sought by Beggs in relation to personal-injury claims as well as litigation for poor craftsmanship when a cupboard door in his mother's fitted kitchen fell off, damaging a cooker in the process. He was a champion for any cause, and had once explained to Bache that the law was there to protect the individual from large organisations, the State and the police. This was Beggs the crusader, battling as the underdog for fair play and accountability.

Interestingly enough, Beggs was rather less than truthful when he spoke of his campaign to purchase his flat in Doon Place some years previously. What he told Bache was that he had fought tooth and nail to secure the purchase of the flat from a Labour council who were against selling off their housing assets, but in the process had found himself in a legal battle with the very authority he had been working for as a housing officer. His position was untenable, and that was his reason for leaving that employment and seeking a career change.

There was a modicum of truth in the story in that he had indeed taken an action against the council after he was refused the option to purchase, but he had conveniently failed to mention his attack on Brian McQuillan in 1991 and his subsequent three-year incarceration.

The emphasis Beggs placed on securing the property at Bellfield for his return from prison was, I suspect, not entirely based on making a sound financial investment, nor, for that matter, a deep desire to put down roots. First, I cannot believe even Beggs could ever imagine being accepted by his immediate neighbours, many of whom had witnessed that distressing day back in July 1991 when McQuillan had leapt from the first-floor window.

Nor do I believe that Beggs was in the perfect place to service his needs in relation to employment or further education. On his release from prison, he would return to the flat in July 1994 with neither a job nor a placement at university. Ideally, Glasgow would have been the obvious place in which to settle where there were more opportunities to further both aspirations.

So why was he adamant that he had to buy this property? Why was he content to live a full 20 minutes' drive away from Glasgow, and among neighbours who knew about his criminal past and would have been hostile towards him?

Was it simply that Ian Beggs had already established some precious memories in that little box bedroom; a hallowed place where he had been able to live out his fantasies and had visions of doing so again. It is possible that there was a ritualistic aspect to his attacks, in that the fantasy would not be complete unless it took place in the spare bedroom. That may not sound like the rational thinking of an educated and articulate man, but, to begin to understand anything about him, one has to make the distinction between Beggs as most people would have seen him on a daily basis and Beggs the killer.

Whatever his reasons, in November 1992, Beggs had applied as a tenant under Section 61 of the Housing (Scotland) Act 1987, for his right to purchase the flat from the local authority. It was a joint application made along with his aunt, Mrs Forsythe, who had apparently been staying in the property from August 1992 at his request. After he had been sentenced to serve six years in prison that September, the rent, which he had been paying by way of benefits, was then taken on by his aunt.

The local authority had refused the application at first and commenced proceedings for recovery of the property. But Beggs was determined, and appealed through the Lands Tribunal for Scotland. They, in turn, ruled that, considering he had only taken up tenancy in April 1990, and had not been living in the flat after his incarceration in July 1991, he had therefore failed to meet the criteria of having been resident in the property for a period totalling not less than two years. Not content with that, and having plenty of time on his hands, Beggs appealed to the Court of Session, who did rule in his favour. They agreed that, in order to prove occupation, the tenant did not have to be physically present, but by keeping his furniture and belongings there he had shown an intention to return. The court then referred the matter back to the tribunal to reconsider their decision.

During consideration, Beggs' aunt and his parents, William and Winifred, were adamant that she had taken up residence as a sort of 'caretaker' for Beggs as he prepared for his return from jail. They would give evidence to support this claim, regardless of the fact that, when the flat was inspected by the tribunal representatives themselves, there were no items of clothing or toiletries suggesting a female living at the address. Even the neighbours living directly beside 2b Doon Place had been asked if they had seen evidence of Mrs Forsythe living at the flat, but they had not. Had his family conveniently lied to assist Beggs in his application?

It must be considered that they had. Even so, the outcome of the tribunal ruled in Ian Beggs' favour, and Kilmarnock and Loudoun District Council, with whom at one time Beggs had fraudulently acquired employment, were then faced with the liability of paying expenses in the matter.

This preoccupation or obsession with the law is another reason that Richard Bache had for believing Beggs to be whiter than white – a model citizen. There were little details which stood out, such as when they would socialise in the pub and, because Beggs would be driving, he would insist on only drinking one pint of beer followed by a pint of shandy, and then a soft drink. He would know exactly the amount of alcohol that would take him over the legal limit to drive, and stay rigidly within that.

Some of Beggs' other little quirks were more irritating than forgivably eccentric, like his timekeeping, for instance. From recollection, Bache was always aware that Beggs would leave almost everything to the last minute, even down to when he was making trips home and had to catch a ferry at a particular time.

When making a trip to the bank, for instance, to either lodge or withdraw cash, Beggs would always arrive within minutes of the branch closing. Not quite living life on the edge perhaps, but it was possibly an exercise in testing himself; seeing exactly how close he could go before disaster or failure was the outcome. We have all felt that little adrenalin rush when stuck in traffic, making our way at a snail's pace towards an appointment we must keep at all costs, the relief palpable when we park our car with seconds to spare. These were probably little games Beggs liked to play for his own amusement; games about control and influence, and the consequences of losing.

On one trip home to Northern Ireland, accompanied by Richard Bache, Beggs chose a convoluted route to the Campbeltown–Ballycastle ferry instead of taking a more direct one as suggested by Bache. In the end, they missed the last boat, and had to stay in the town for the night and travel the next morning. Strangely, though, Beggs was neither concerned nor disappointed. He accepted that it was his fault entirely, a consequence of his poor route choice.

To the police investigating the murder, Richard Bache was invaluable, and not just because he could provide them with an insight into the mind of the killer. Over the period of the weekend of 4–6 December, the time of Wallace's murder, he had actually spoken to Beggs on the telephone. It was during that call that Beggs had bragged about having a sexual encounter with a 'sweet' or 'cute' young man.

According to phone records, the conversation between Bache and Beggs took place just after half-past five in the evening on Sunday, 5 December 1999. It had been initiated from Richard Bache's home telephone to Beggs' mobile number and, according to Bache, he was sure that Ian Beggs had been driving at the time. In his own words, he could hear 'the engine in the background'.

When he asked Beggs where he was, he had replied that he was driving to Edinburgh. As friends do, they spoke generally and Bache asked Beggs what he had got up to the previous evening, a Saturday night. It was then that Beggs said that he had 'got off with a guy'. This was not just a casual meeting Beggs was describing. Something in his voice suggested he was rather pleased with himself, smug even. And there was no mistaking that Beggs was alluding to a sexual encounter.

There was no denying that these two men knew each other well, and, if anyone could ever be described as being a confidant to Beggs, Richard Bache would be that person. During one of the numerous conversations Bache had with police, he was left a little disturbed when they had told him that, save for Beggs' parents, he was undoubtedly one of the closest people to Ian Beggs. A matter of a few weeks later, they amended that observation and told him that he was, in fact, *the* closest person to Beggs.

There was no cause for Bache to celebrate. If anything, he began to feel the pressure of the enormity of the situation in terms of what he may or may not have been privy to, albeit unwittingly. During our conversation, he described how, over the six-month period when he was assisting the police, he began to regard himself as 'the ring bearer', as in the Tolkien trilogy. He was the unfortunate person burdened with the evil that was Beggs, and trusted with delivering it to its ultimate end.

If the timeline the police had decided upon was correct, and they were fairly confident that it was, then the conversation the two men had that Sunday evening had taken place after Beggs had brutally murdered Barry Wallace and possibly even after he had dismembered his body. Evidence would suggest that the body parts had been dumped in Loch Lomond sometime before the morning of 6 December. When Richard Bache would reflect upon what had seemed an everyday conversation between two mates, he would realise that, as they spoke, Beggs may have been driving along the road to Balmaha pier with the body of his 'sweet' young man already cut into pieces and wrapped up in plastic bags.

10

The Puppeteer

A recurring theme throughout the Beggs story is the role his parents adopted after each of their son's crimes came to light. First, family members appeared to close ranks and dig in for the inevitable onslaught by either press or police and, instead of remaining tight-lipped, were quite vocal in his defence. In 1987, they made no bones about the fact that they were convinced police had made a horrible mistake and arrested the wrong man, and then again in 1991 they were in no doubt of his innocence, to the extent that they approached and engaged handwriting experts to assist in attempting to cast doubt on the integrity of certain police officers involved in investigating the case. Whatever their motives, they appeared somewhat detached from reality, taking the loving, protective parents role much too far. In many ways, their relationship appears incongruous, and not the type of background we expect a killer such as Beggs to have come from. Or was it?

It has been suggested that William and Winifred Beggs may have gone well beyond what any child would expect of their parents in terms of help in times of crisis. They were two well-educated individuals with, I assume, a modicum of common sense, and still, when details of the Barry Wallace murder emerged with their son identified as the prime suspect, they chose to believe he was a victim of some huge conspiracy. They had also been described as a deeply religious family, their Christian values and convictions central to the way they lived their lives. Yet, here was a man who had broken the most coveted of all commandments – 'thou shalt not kill' – not once but possibly several times, and still they chose to ignore the overwhelming evidence and assist their eldest boy in any way they could.

Throughout the Wallace murder investigation, allegations were made which suggested that, over the period of the week after 6 December, when the limbs had been discovered at Loch Lomond, Beggs' parents and his aunt, Mrs Forsythe, had travelled from Northern Ireland to Scotland, and had bought cleaning and decorating supplies in a local store in Kilmarnock, and may well have helped Beggs redecorate the spare bedroom.

It was something that the police would address later when they had dealt with Ian Beggs himself, but the implications were huge. Had they willingly and knowingly tried to pervert the course of justice by helping to sanitise a murder scene? Had Ian Beggs come running home to mummy with a tale of woe similar to when he had murdered Barry Oldham, pleading for help to hide his 'mistake'? And, if he had, did they then choose to try to keep the matter within the family circle and not contact the authorities?

It would eventually be up to Kilmarnock Fiscal John Watt at the end of Beggs' trial to consider what to do with the couple, who were both in their mid-sixties, and the aunt, who was 75 years old at the time. There has to be a point when parents decide that enough is enough, and accept that they cannot go on being responsible for the actions of their children. Still, even during the Wallace trial, William Beggs senior refused to believe what he was hearing day in and day out, even calling a local radio station in Scotland, clearly incensed at the media coverage of the trial which, in his opinion, was vilifying his son. Even then, upon hearing the strength of the evidence, he still proclaimed his son's innocence. Admirable to say the least, but extremely foolish and misguided.

If they had only accepted that their son was a psychopathic killer who had preyed on defenceless individuals, then they could have done what any Christian person would have done – convince him to plead guilty and spare the Wallace family a trial, and to accept his fate as a sinner in the eyes of God. They must have been torn between adherence to their faith and what they saw as their duty to their first-born child. What part of God's laws did the Beggs family wish to adhere to, and what parts did they choose to ignore? No one can criticise them for being supportive of their son; they were there for him throughout each and every sordid episode of his life, and I have no doubt he takes great comfort from them and from his siblings. But where was their compassion for his victims and their families?

Even more bizarre was the fact that, directly after the conclusion of her son's trial, Winifred Beggs approached her solicitor, Tony Caher, from the law firm Campbell and Caher in Lisburn, and put in motion a writ of summons against the Chief Constable of Strathclyde Police with regard to wrongful detention and false imprisonment in January 2000 at Grosvenor Road Police Station in Belfast. This, of course, referred to the arrest of both of Beggs' parents and his elderly aunt for questioning in relation to perverting the course of justice in the Wallace murder, a matter which was still being investigated.

The writ, which had been lodged at Belfast High Court, stated: 'The Plaintiff's claim is for damages for personal injuries, loss and damage, distress and inconvenience sustained and suffered by the Plaintiff by reason and the wrongful detention, false imprisonment and trespass to the Plaintiff's person committed by the Defendant, by his servants and agents in and about January 2000.'

The arrests had been made for purposes of interview, and

after the six-hour detention period all three had been released without charge but informed that matters would be reported to the Procurator Fiscal. They did, however, have their fingerprints taken along with mouth swabs for DNA, in accordance with normal practice for anyone detained for a recordable offence.

I am at a loss as to why Mrs Beggs, having already been through so much with the media circus surrounding her son's trial, would even want to consider raising her head above the parapet and placing herself in the spotlight. As soon as Beggs had been convicted and sent to prison, the story would have naturally faded away to be replaced by something else. But I can't help thinking about the influence Ian may have had over his parents, and how he would have insisted they take issue with police, coaching them towards a legal action. After all, he had plenty of experience in that field.

Interestingly, in November 2002, only a month before a planned three-day hearing was to begin, they abandoned their writ.

There were those who believed they knew the Beggs family well, and who, after reading the more graphic accounts of the Wallace murder, began to question how someone who had been the product of such a loving family could have done such a thing to a fellow human being. Why, if all that was being said was true, had Ian Beggs turned out so bad?

It is rather convenient for us to believe that violent individuals are often a product of broken homes, dysfunctional family lives and a less-than-adequate education. Somehow, we are more comfortable if we can easily compartmentalise those who commit crimes of violence against others. The rationale, of course, is that reasonably intelligent individuals from a solid family background will have acquired the proper tools with which to calibrate their moral compass, their reasoned decision-making therefore setting them apart from criminals and thugs.

From the time of Barry Oldham's murder and thereafter, when Beggs was released on appeal, there had been a considerable amount of articles written in the papers about his family background and, by all accounts, Beggs certainly seemed to be the exception to the rule.

The Beggs family had originally set up house in Lurgan, County Armagh, and were valued members of the local Baptist congregation. William Ian Frederick was born on 4 October 1963, the first of five children, and spent his early years in Lurgan before the family relocated to a large, detached rural house close to the town of Moira in County Down when he was in his early teens.

The small town of Moira was only a few miles away from where they had been living in Lurgan, but in terms of attitude and integration between two opposing communities the two towns couldn't have been further apart. This part of County Down was fairly affluent, and commuting to Belfast and nearby Lisburn was relatively painless due to easy access to the M1 motorway at the bottom of the town's main street.

The community spirit in this small town was such that local butchers, bakers and convenience stores seldom suffered loss of trade, even though the large multinationals had sprung up only a matter of minutes away off the main motorway link. A great sense of civic pride existed here with commercial buildings, homes and gardens being well presented throughout the year, regardless of the challenges of the Northern Irish weather, earning the community various accolades for 'best-kept' small town or village on more than one occasion.

The end of the 1960s in Northern Ireland saw the beginning of civil and political unrest, eventually making way for murder, mayhem and destruction in the following decades, a turbulent time which became known as the 'Troubles'.

At the age of 11, transfer test behind him, the young Beggs became a pupil at the Quaker-based Friends School in Lisburn. The school had a rich history, stemming from its beginnings in 1774 and its first headmaster, John Gough. By the start of the 1900s, it was to serve as one of Northern Ireland's leading grammar schools, enrolling pupils from all denominations, not just Quakers.

Detective Sergeant Andy Sproule had spoken to Mr Arthur Chapman, who had been Beggs' former headmaster at Friends, and the picture he had painted was one of a studious and conscientious pupil who at the end of an 'unremarkable' seven years had achieved nine O-levels and two A-levels. But it wasn't his academic achievements that would set him apart from his peers.

In an article written by journalist Craig Watson in the *Herald* newspaper in October 2003, comments made by a former pupil in the same school year as Beggs suggested he was anything but unremarkable, but not necessarily in the same context. According to this source, Beggs had been treated with almost 'blanket hostility' by his fellow pupils, to the point that nobody was keen to sit beside him, particularly the females. He described him as a 'creep', and in a poignant comment said, 'It sounds amazing now but we actually said at the time that he was the sort of person we would read about in the papers one day. We knew he was screwed up.'

Regardless of his personality issues, Beggs was seen to have a flare for languages, something which he would continue to excel at throughout the rest of his life, becoming fluent in French and German and travelling extensively in and around Europe.

Even at school age, when young men and women should be socialising together and enjoying their teenage years, the serious, almost reclusive Beggs developed a taste for politics both locally and nationally, initially following his family tradition of supporting the Ulster Unionist agenda, but later edging towards the Democratic Unionist Party (DUP). His interest in local politics may have been bolstered as a result of his introduction to David Trimble by his uncle, Fred Crowe,

Looking into the eyes of a killer – William Frederick Ian Beggs.

Above: The young Beggs attended Friends' School in Lisburn, County Antrim. © *Mirrorpix*

Below: Beggs' flat was located in this building in Kilmarnock. © *Mirrorpix*

Above: Following the discovery of the limbs in Loch Lomond, police officers search the east banks of the Loch.   © *PA Photos*

Below: Detective Chief Inspector Jim Porteous, Detective Superintendent John Geates and Chief Superintendent Bill Campbell from Strathclyde Police launch an appeal to the public for information about the murder of Barry Wallace.   © *PA Photos*

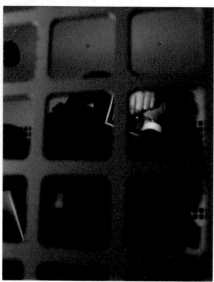

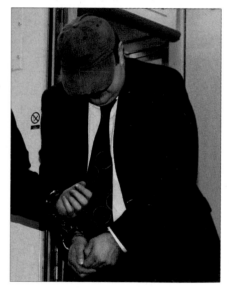

Above: Beggs is driven from Edinburgh High Court to begin his life sentence for the murder of Barry Wallace. © *PA Photos*

Below left: Beggs shields his face from the press as he is taken away.

© *Mirrorpix*

Below right: Beggs arrives for an appeal against his conviction for the murder of Barry Wallace. © *PA Photos* his mother's brother, himself a Unionist stalwart who was to serve as Mayor of Craigavon on two separate occasions.

Around the time the introduction was made, David Trimble, a barrister and lecturer by profession, had left behind the hard-line Vanguard Party and moved towards mainstream Unionist politics. Such was his standing in the Ulster Unionist Party that in 1995 he became the party leader, and was one of the key figures in carrying forward the peace process in Northern Ireland, resulting in the signing of the Good Friday Agreement.

But it seems Ian Beggs was more inclined to favour the extremes in politics and aligned himself with the DUP, signing up to one or more of their more controversial campaigns, including an all-out assault on the gay community in the form of 'Save Ulster from Sodomy'.

In a country in the midst of conflict with two opposing factions trading blow for murderous blow daily on the streets, Northern Ireland politics had little time to draw breath and consider normal social issues such as unemployment, housing and health, never mind discuss matters which always drew controversy such as the decriminalisation of homosexuality. Acts of homosexuality between consenting adults had been decriminalised in England and Wales since 1967, but not in Northern Ireland or Scotland.

In 1974, there had been a concerted effort to have those reforms extended to include Northern Ireland with the creation of the Campaign for Homosexual Law Reform, a bridge too far according to firebrand DUP MP Ian Paisley. The self-styled leader of the Free Presbyterian Church and DUP head never really divorced religion from politics and saw it as his moral duty to preserve the teachings of the Bible. His interpretation was both literal and rigid and he clearly regarded homosexuality as a sin. In 1977, he embarked on the 'Save Ulster from Sodomy' campaign, branding the practice of homosexuality as an abomination which undermined the Christian beliefs and aspirations of the Protestant people of the Province. As far as his political opponents were concerned, it was just another example of Paisley's extreme intolerance of all things outside of his own beliefs and culture.

Despite his objections, homosexual acts were decriminalised in Northern Ireland in 1982. Although in more recent times the DUP has been seen to be the party which has moved the most towards breaking down political and religious barriers during the implementation of the Good Friday Agreement, as late as June 2008 DUP MP Iris Robinson, the wife of First Minister Peter Robinson, spoke out against homosexuality during a radio interview. During that interview, she even suggested that homosexuality was a 'condition' which could be cured with the intervention of a therapist. Needless to say, there was outrage from the gay community and beyond up and down the country. It would also not be the last occasion that Mrs Robinson would embarrass her husband, as on 6 January 2010 a story was released to the press that earlier in 2009 Mrs Robinson had attempted suicide after admitting to her husband that she had been having an extra-marital affair with a local businessman, a young man 30 years her junior. Some would be quick to accuse her of having double standards, and others more sympathetic in the plight of a vulnerable female fallen foul of an old-fashioned affair of the heart. When details of her financial impropriety were to follow over the next few days, though, all sympathy disappeared.

There have also been suggestions that Beggs had come under the notice of the paramilitaries in Northern Ireland and, as a result, had chosen to move to the mainland to escape summary justice. According to some newspapers, it was a senior figure in the Ulster Volunteer Force (UVF) in the Lurgan area who had given Beggs the ultimatum, after he had been found lurking around certain schools and paying attention to young boys. I have not been able to establish whether there was ever any truth in the matter, but paramilitary groups like the UVF, UDA and the IRA were known to appoint themselves as judge, jury and sometime executioners in the areas they controlled. To lay claim to having rid an area of a suspected paedophile would have raised their esteem among the local community, and would have been difficult to refute.

I suspect, though, that Ian Beggs had his own reasons for wanting to study away from home in England. Northern

Ireland is a small country in comparison to England, Scotland or Wales for that matter, boasting a population of just 1.5 million people. There are few places in the country one can go without coming across a neighbour, relative or acquaintance; a place where secrets are hard to keep and reputations travel faster than the train service. It would have been extremely difficult for Beggs to hide his sexuality in such a parochial place. Equally, it would prove difficult for his violent tendencies to go unnoticed among an even smaller gay community, already defined by a matter of a few pubs and clubs within Belfast city centre.

The Northern Ireland Gay Rights Association (NIGRA) was to make life even more difficult for Beggs when details of his exploits became known to them. The association was more of a pressure group than a fully fledged organisation with paid-up members and regular meetings. They were, however, committed to providing those in the GLBT community with a platform and a voice with which to lobby support for important issues such as the fight against Paisley's 'Save Ulster from Sodomy' campaign. The little newsletter they published, *Upstart*, which kept their target audience aware of ongoing issues, among many other things, was where they first printed an image of Ian Beggs along with a warning to the reader to avoid him at all costs. According to them, he was a danger to all gay men, and, for those who already had the misfortune to know him, they were asked to pass the message on to their friends on the scene.

I recently made contact with a male of similar age to Ian Beggs, who was, and still is, fairly well known within the Ulster gay scene. This male, who prefers to remain anonymous, professed to having known Beggs, albeit through a mutual acquaintance. According to this source, it was well known within the gay community that Ian Beggs, in his senior years at Friends school, had attacked another student on a camping trip, cutting him on the legs with a razor blade while they shared a sleeping bag. When I asked him how he was sure that the story was true, he told me that the person who had been assaulted was a close friend of his and he could vouch for his honesty.

With his choices narrowed down somewhat, Beggs chose to enrol at Teesside Polytechnic in the north-east to study public administration and, over the next few years, lived in various student digs until he eventually ended up in Princes Road. During that period at Teesside, Beggs was actively involved with the Federation of Conservative Students (FCS) along with many of his friends, including Lucinda Geldard, the daughter of then Conservative MP for Uxbridge Sir Michael Shersby. The FCS was, in effect, the student wing of the British Conservative Party, and, although it initially provided a link between the student movement and the party, it quickly found its own identity. Many had thought of it purely as a means of networking for like-minded people, more of a social club than a serious association with its own very real agenda. Beggs was different, though, and his involvement was whole-hearted.

Such was his commitment to the FCS that he was elected regional chairman, and most who knew him at the time were certain he would find his career in political life as an MP. He did actually make it to Downing Street, not as an MP, but as a guest for a Burns' Night Supper, an event which further fuelled his ambition to become part of the bigger political picture.

According to some, the catalyst for bringing those ambitions to a halt was the signing of the Anglo–Irish Agreement in 1985. Although the agreement had been voted in by a large majority in the House of Commons, it remained one of Prime Minister Margaret Thatcher's less popular decisions during her period in office. From a Unionist point of view, the idea that the Republic of Ireland would be involved, albeit in an advisory role, in the affairs of Northern Ireland was nothing less than a sell-out, an unforgivable act of treachery according to Ulster Unionist Party leader James Molyneaux. But it was Ian Paisley who was the most vocal opponent to the deal, attending mass rallies and urging Unionist voters to organise strikes and take part in civil disobedience.

I suspect it wouldn't have been much of a dilemma for Beggs whether to agree with the majority of the Conservative Party and support Thatcher's decision, or to pin his colours to Paisley's anti-agreement campaign. He had always aligned himself with the extremes in Unionism, and would have agreed that signing up to any such deal was moving uncomfortably close to achieving the goals of the IRA and delivering a united Ireland.

There were mass resignations from the House of Commons by all Unionist MPs, and Beggs felt more than a little disillusioned and confused by the Conservative Party's policies. Living in England hadn't dampened his fervour for home-grown issues, particularly when they involved a potential threat to the strength of the Union and the Protestant way of life. But times were changing, and, if the governments of Britain and the Republic of Ireland were lending their weight to a process of inclusion and mediation, then it was probably only a matter of time before an all-inclusive agreement would be on the table. Beggs may have sensed the changes coming and accepted he could have little impact upon them, regardless of where he practised his politics.

The only real person who could offer any form of insight into who Beggs the 'adult' was would be Richard Bache. As we have seen, their friendship started in earnest around the end of 1995, when both men worked and studied alongside each other at Paisley University, Beggs completing his Master's project and Bache teaching in the same department. The two men often travelled to and from the university together, and socialised frequently in both Edinburgh and Glasgow.

From the outset, Richard Bache is clear that, during their many conversations over the next three years, Ian Beggs would describe his sex life as being 'eclectic'. Not necessarily a word I or anyone else would use, other than to describe our taste in music perhaps. But Beggs had used it in a wholly different context, to make the point that he wasn't particularly fussy whether his sexual partners were male or female. He was very clear when the matter was discussed that he was not, however, a homosexual. According to him, everything, including one's sexual orientation, was a matter of free will, and that, in fact, there was no such thing as homosexuality; instead, we choose to sleep with members of the same sex because we want to, not because we are intrinsically predisposed to do so.

Reading between the lines as such, Beggs is reluctant to admit to being a slave to his sexuality, having no control over who he is attracted to. Even though he attempts to hide behind this flawed philosophy, his track record with women is negligible. Throughout this period, Bache was aware that Beggs would have had one or more relationships with men in particular, but he could only remember details of one female, a German girl by the name of Brigit, whom Beggs himself had labelled as his girlfriend. There had, of course, been Lucinda Geldard, his fellow student at Teesside Polytechnic, but their relationship was possibly more platonic than anything else, even though she had been described by the press as a 'girlfriend'.

It was clear that Beggs was comfortable confiding in Bache, although, when I spoke to Bache, he accepted, after learning who his companion really was and what he had been capable of, that what he had been told by Ian Beggs was possibly one-third truth, one-third fiction and the last third a mixture of both. Of course, the more he questioned whether he actually knew the real Ian Beggs, the more he realised that he knew only the part that Beggs had been willing to reveal to him, and not what was really underneath.

I cannot help but wonder whether, if their relationship had been a physical one, sharing a degree of intimacy as such, rather than just a friendship, Beggs would have been able to sustain it for a period as long as three years. I suspect not, simply because I believe that with passion and intimacy comes an abandonment of secrets and inhibitions – our true desires and instincts revealed within the sexual act.

From what we know of Beggs during the latter part of the Eighties, and of the accusations that he had been responsible for around 14 incidents involving slashing men, it is clear that in certain circumstances he follows a pattern of behaviour. Invariably, that behaviour comes about when he is presented with what he perceives to be an opportunity for sex, albeit with partners who are either subdued and unwilling or unsuspecting. If Richard Bache had been identified by Beggs as a potential sexual partner, then he, too, may have experienced the penchant Beggs had for cutting people.

In Bache, however, Beggs had met someone he believed to be his intellectual equal, and with whom he could discuss matters which were more important to him than sex and the pursuit of a partner. To that end, Beggs in turn had to secure their relationship as he saw it, by fending off any possible suitors for Bache in the best way he could, by manipulation and intervention. He was desperate to keep Richard Bache to himself as his sounding board and his trusty travelling companion.

It wouldn't be apparent to Bache at the time that this was the case, but retrospectively he could see exactly how and when it had been done. In one particular case, Bache had met a guy in Edinburgh and, as they found each other attractive, he had given him his telephone number. He waited for a phone call, but it never came. It wasn't that he had read the wrong signals, although at the time he could not find any other plausible explanation; it was the fact that Ian Beggs had travelled to Edinburgh to warn the other person off his friend Richard.

Beggs also sabotaged a dinner party which Richard was hosting with one particular guest in mind; it was an opportunity to get to know this man and possibly strike up a relationship. Unfortunately, Bache confided in Beggs, who then engineered it so that it appeared that Bache had snubbed this man by not inviting him. When the evening came and his most important guest didn't turn up, Bache assumed that he was the one who had been snubbed.

Ian Beggs was also very vocal about how he disliked some of Richard's friends, and how in his opinion they didn't measure up. In contrast, he would go out of his way to help

Richard Bache, whether it was giving him lifts in his car to and from university, or moving furniture from his old flat into his new one. In his own words, Bache says that Ian Beggs was 'courting his friendship'.

But it was all very much part of a big game for Beggs, who liked to be the one pulling the strings, the puppet master, controlling people with his sleight of hand and manoeuvring them into position. He wasn't concerned about the consequences of his games because he felt nothing for the people involved. In fact, it may have been that he was amused by the outcomes of many of his little interventions. When Richard Bache looks back dispassionately at the type of 'friendship' the two men had, it becomes all too obvious that it was very one-sided indeed.

11
Opportunity Knocks

With just the limbs to examine, the police could only speculate as to how Barry Wallace had actually died, and it was proving difficult to find the torso. The searches taking place at Loch Lomond and the surrounding areas were still ongoing.

The wounds to the arms and legs had been determined as being caused post mortem as a result of the dismemberment, and could not provide any clues as to the cause of death. There was, however, a puncture mark on one of the arms, which when examined closely resembled that which would be left by a hypodermic needle. The position of the mark on the arm suggested that, at the time it had been made, Barry would have had to have both his arms placed behind his back in order to expose that area of skin. It was therefore extremely unlikely he would have inflicted that mark upon himself. Again, though, without the torso and the major organs, identifying any toxins in the body would be difficult.

From examination of the head, it appeared that at sometime during the evening Barry had been punched in the face, probably more than once, causing bruises and swelling. That was about as much as could be determined, although it was plain to see that, whatever had happened, Barry's death was a violent one.

The punch in the face had probably been enough to subdue the 18-year-old, who by all accounts had consumed a fair amount of alcohol that evening. It was then that handcuffs had been applied to both his wrists and his ankles. Such was the ferocity of his struggle against being restrained that pathologist Dr Fernie would later describe the wounds as some of the worst he had seen, even in comparison to what would be expected from an intoxicated person who was 'forcibly' resisting arrest.

When the missing torso was eventually recovered from Loch Lomond in January 2000, police hoped that the question as to how Barry had died could finally be answered. An initial examination revealed that he had been subjected to an almost indescribable ordeal; obvious bruising to his anus and rectal area was compatible with a 'sexual assault of considerable force'.

Unfortunately, even with an extensive forensic post mortem, the finding on the actual cause of death was inconclusive. It may simply have been that such was the shock he suffered at the hands of a prolonged and brutal attack that Barry had died from heart failure. Or, as was also suggested, he may have been asphyxiated due to the position he had been placed in during the sexual assault, with his face pushed down into the bedclothes. Neither explanation would be any comfort to his family or friends; the pain and suffering Barry would have been subjected to was already beyond their comprehension.

Unfortunately, there were more revelations to come.

As if the details of Barry's assault were not horrific enough, already painting a very graphic picture of the torturous last few hours of the young man's life, the way in which Beggs dismembered his lifeless body was even more disturbing. It seems that, once again, as in the Barry Oldham murder, Ian Beggs was ill-equipped to deal with the task in hand, and had to revert to using a large kitchen knife to cut off the limbs and head from the torso. The cutting up of a body is in itself an indescribable horror. Even when it is performed as part of a post-mortem, as required by law in most cases of unexplained sudden death, we are not comfortable at the thought of the remains of our loved ones being subjected to such an invasive process. I cannot begin to imagine the distress the Wallace family must have felt when they were told that Beggs, in his attempt to complete his gory task with just a knife, and finding it slow and arduous, had resorted to cutting through the larger bones a fraction of the way, and then snapping them apart with his bare hands.

I know we must consider that when life is extinct our bodies can no longer feel pain. But the manner in which Beggs dealt with Barry's body a short time after his death, quite possibly when his life blood was still warm in his veins, is beyond the pale. It is a desecration which adds insurmountable pain and suffering, not to Barry, but to the living victims, the Wallace family.

What is even more disconcerting, though, is when one remembers that it was only a matter of a few hours after Beggs had cut up his victim when Richard Bache had called him from his home telephone and asked him how his weekend had been. During that conversation, which lasted for around ten minutes, Bache had not detected any signs of stress or anxiety from his friend. Quite the contrary, Bache would later say that, in his opinion, Beggs had been his 'usual self'.

Just how detached was Ian Beggs? How can one human being be immersed in such bloody carnage in what should be an overwhelmingly stressful situation and then carry on a totally normal conversation a matter of a few hours later? It would be details such as this which would earn Beggs his title as a 'monster'.

There was obviously physical evidence recovered from the search of Beggs' flat at Doon Place and, hopefully, some of that would yield DNA or fingerprints which could tie in Barry's presence at the flat. Despite that, though, the police still had to piece together a timeline of Barry's movements on the evening of 4 December into the morning of 5 December, and those of Ian Beggs.

Physical evidence alone is not necessarily enough to prove that a suspect has killed someone. One still has to determine whether that suspect has had the opportunity to do so in the time frame and geography relevant to the crime. If, for instance, police were to recover items from a property which is believed to be a crime scene, and those items are found to have traces of a victim's blood on them, all they can safely say is that the victim may well have been in that property at sometime or another. There can be numerous explanations as to why and when a victim may have been at the crime scene or, for that matter, why their blood or DNA may be present there. It may be that they had been frequent visitors to the property and, during one of those visits, may have injured themselves and left an item behind bearing their blood. It may also be the case that the suspect and the victim came in close contact outside of the suggested crime scene, and there was a transfer of blood from one to the other. In the words of renowned criminologist Edmond Locard, 'every contact leaves a trace', a widely accepted concept in crime scene investigation which acts both for and against a suspect's explanation of events.

The investigation team have to close off any routes a suspect may choose to present as part of his defence, and marry the physical evidence up with the circumstantial in order to arrive at a credible explanation of events which any jury will see is both possible and probable.

It was no different when the police were building their case against Beggs. The burning question was where he had been on the evening of 4 December, and whether he had had the opportunity to meet up with Barry Wallace, take him back to the flat and carry out the murder. In a small town such as Kilmarnock, where Barry was well enough known and liked, it wasn't proving difficult to find witnesses who would come forward to help police trace his last movements. And, if they had seen Barry as he walked around the town centre that night, perhaps they had seen him with his killer.

It was Saturday, 4 December 1999, and Barry Wallace had already made plans to finish off the rest of his Christmas shopping in the town and then meet up with his friend Lewis Caddis, whom he worked alongside at the local Tesco supermarket. There was to be his work's party later, but there was plenty of time for a few beers before that. When he had turned up at the store to make the arrangement with Lewis, who had been working a later shift, he had bumped into his parents, Ian and Christine. That was the last time his father would see him alive, although he would speak to him again on the telephone as Barry sat eating the meal his mum had cooked for him before he was to go out that evening.

The Christmas party culture is such that it is often the only opportunity for employees, regardless of position or rank, to come together and let their hair down in a neutral environment. There is inevitably too much drink taken, and the odd little indiscretion is best forgotten come the return to work the next day. It wasn't necessarily Barry's first choice of venue for his precious weekend's entertainment, as he had said that he would have been happy to go out with his pals as normal. His colleagues had other ideas, though, and he was eventually cajoled into going.

Barry was a fairly shy teenager by all accounts, although his obvious good looks and athletic physique would have made him popular with the young females. He was from a happy home with strong family bonds, and would regularly meet up with his dad and younger brother Colin for a few beers after work at the Howard Park Hotel in Kilmarnock. On leaving school, Barry had aspirations to join the Navy and see the world, but when offered a full-time job at Tesco in Kilmarnock he chose to stay in his home town. At that point in his life, Barry must have believed that there was plenty of time to make huge career choices, so why make them now when he could enjoy his youth and settle down sometime later in the future?

Even though Barry had been the reluctant partygoer, he seemed to enter into the spirit of things as the night went on at the Foxbar Hotel. He was never usually one to overindulge, but clearly he did that evening, and was described by other revellers as being really quite drunk. But he was a normal 18-year-old, fearless and full of life, and not worried about the consequences of a full-blown hangover. He mustn't have wanted the night to end, as he had refused a lift home from one of the girls who had been driving, deciding instead to walk into town to the Expo nightclub.

The route which Barry took that evening was reasonably easy to plot. One young man in particular, Graham Boax, was eager to come forward to place himself and Barry at a taxi rank in the town centre. He was keen to tell the police that not only had he spoken to Barry, but he had actually had an argument which had ended up with the two young men trading punches. In light of what had happened to Barry over the next 24 hours, Graham Boax must have been relieved when the police had dismissed him as a suspect in the case. Their argument was a drunken disagreement between old friends, and had been resolved almost as quickly as it had started, the pair making up before Barry moved on. Nevertheless, for obvious reasons, it had to be established whether Barry had sustained any injuries from the unco-ordinated exchanges. According to Boax, Barry had not been cut by any of the punches, nor had he seen any blood on his face.

One other witness, Wesley Kirkland, who had also seen Barry in the vicinity of the Expo club at around 1.45am, had stated that he had not seen any signs of physical injury, and certainly not any blood. From that point on, there were no other sightings of Barry. He had more or less vanished from the street.

One must then consider that Barry met up with someone

who offered him a lift home, or possibly the promise of a few more drinks at a party. Whatever the scenario, that person was likely to have been Barry's killer.

As Barry was chatting and dancing the night away, Ian Beggs was in Edinburgh gate-crashing a fancy-dress party being hosted by 26-year-old Berengere Lecouvreur. There were numerous house parties being held throughout the month of December that year all across the UK. After all, this was to be the last Christmas of the twentieth century and the prelude to the eagerly anticipated Millennium celebrations. But this fancy-dress party was primarily a birthday celebration, and when Beggs arrived almost an hour before any other guests at the address in Portobello, and on the back of an invite from a work colleague, he was not exactly welcome. The host was even more bewildered because Beggs hadn't even made the effort to dress for the occasion. This was in total contrast to a few months earlier when Beggs had attended a fancy-dress function arranged by a team member within Sykes call centre dressed as a giant condom, and draped all over in smaller condoms. He had made quite an effort then and quite an impression, too.

Throughout the birthday party that evening, Beggs mentioned to a few others he knew from Sykes that he wasn't drinking as he intended to drive back to Kilmarnock sometime around midnight. He was immediately singled out by some as a potential designated driver and good for a lift home. One witness and also a colleague of Beggs', Andrew

Aird, was confident that his workmate had left just before midnight. In fact, he had looked for him in order to cadge a lift, but when he couldn't see him among the party revellers, he had to phone a friend to come and get him instead. That call was made at 11.55pm according to his phone records.

It was over 70 miles back to Kilmarnock. The duration of the journey depended very much on the amount of traffic, the speed of the car and how direct a route was taken. But this was a journey Ian Beggs was well used to, travelling to and from his place of work on a regular basis, but usually during busier times of the day. When the police took it upon themselves to replicate the journey, travelling the most direct route at reasonable speeds, it was clear that it would have taken somewhere in the region of an hour-and-a-half, give or take a few minutes.

If Andrew Aird's recollection was accurate, and there was no reason to assume otherwise, then Beggs, having left Edinburgh around midnight to half-past, could have arrived comfortably in Kilmarnock at sometime close to 1.30–2.00am. That was around the same time Barry Wallace was last spotted in the town centre.

So now the investigation team could say that it was possible that Ian Beggs could have been present in Kilmarnock town centre at the same time as Barry's disappearance. Unless he could come up with a credible alibi that he was somewhere else at that time, they had established that he had the opportunity to abduct and murder Barry Wallace.

Yet another piece of the puzzle had fitted into place. The team had now covered the aspect of opportunity and, with the mountain of physical evidence recovered from the flat, they were sure that they could establish that Beggs certainly had the means with which to murder Barry. The very last piece of the puzzle was identifying a motive for the attack, if indeed there was one.

It may have seemed like a moot point to many, bearing in mind the type of offending history Ian Beggs already had. The Barry Oldham murder in 1987, and the two counts of wounding the same year, along with the attack on Brian McQuillan, were all in the public domain, and went a long way to proving that Beggs was a violent offender preying on men. But it was no secret that McQuillan and Oldham had been practising homosexuals, and quite clearly Barry Wallace did not fit into that category. Why then would Beggs have risked approaching a young heterosexual male to try to coax him to come home with him and then assault him? Why not just pick someone up from a gay bar and engage in consensual sex?

The answer eventually came from a man by the name of Kenneth Petrie, who had known Ian Beggs for around two years, both men frequenting the gay clubs and bars in the city, but particularly Number 18 Sauna in the Newtown Bar in Dublin Street, where they had first met.

First, and quite significantly, Kenneth Petrie made himself known to police and offered up information in the form of a statement to Detective Constable James Robertson. It couldn't have been easy for Petrie to make the approach, knowing full well the negative relationship the police had with the gay community in general, and that in doing so he would have to be open and honest about his own sexuality. In the words of Detective Constable Robertson, Petrie was 'very timid, very quiet' when they first met one afternoon at the Newtown Bar. He was committed to helping police with their enquiries, though, and agreed to return with them to Gayfield Police Station in the city and provide a formal statement.

So that his statement would be in context, Petrie first admitted to being a gay man and that he had frequented the many establishments linked with the Edinburgh gay scene for a period of around three years. In the statement, Petrie recounted conversations between himself and Beggs, and certain revelations Beggs had made as to how and why he preferred to pick up straight men from straight bars, as opposed to gay men from gay bars. There was enough detail in the affidavit for detectives immediately to realise the significance of what they were being told.

What Kenneth Petrie had described was a plausible explanation as to how Ian Beggs would identify and select an unwitting victim, render them incapable and then carry out whatever depraved act he desired. It certainly explained what may have happened to Barry Wallace. Perhaps in Beggs' mind he felt that an inebriated straight male who was sexually assaulted might fear coming forward to make a formal complaint due to the embarrassment and the potential ridicule or, for that matter, the possibility of having his own sexuality questioned. We already know that it had happened before, when Beggs was alleged to have attacked numerous males with razor blades and they had been reluctant to come forward fearing being outed as being gay themselves. It was just possible that he considered this a winning formula which enabled him to carry out his sick sexual fantasies without fear of attracting police notice. Whatever the explanation, his encounter with Barry Wallace had gone one step further.

Unfortunately for all concerned, Kenneth Petrie died before the case came to court, and his evidence had to be given by way of the content of his statement, which would not afford the defence an opportunity to cross-examine him. It wasn't ideal for either the defence or the prosecution as, by all accounts, Petrie would have made a compelling and plausible witness. Nevertheless, the significance of the insight he provided into Beggs the sexual predator was substantial, and the police now had a motive for the murder of Barry Wallace.

12

No Stone Unturned

By putting distance between himself and Scotland, and choosing of his own free will to surface in a country he knew had strict extradition laws, we can assume that Beggs had done so in order to give himself time to think through his predicament and arrive at a plausible defence, should he be arrested and returned to Scotland to face any charges.

If we look back at his trial for the murder of Barry Oldham in 1987, Beggs had pleaded not guilty on the grounds of self-defence – a straight man fending off a sexual assault from an openly gay male, but causing fatal injuries to that male in doing so. He used exactly the same defence during his trial for the assault on Brian McQuillan in 1991. His denials that he was a gay man were unwavering, but at every opportunity he would balance that with a statement that, although he was heterosexual, he was in no way a homophobe, which could be considered another possible motive for attacking gay men.

In the Barry Wallace murder, however, because of the obvious marks left by the handcuffs, and the clear signs of a violent sexual assault, Beggs must have realised that the only possible way to defend himself against an allegation of premeditated murder would have been to suggest that the sex between him and Wallace had been consensual, and that unfortunately Wallace had died a natural death during or after the act.

Only then – fearing he would spend the rest of his life in prison for the brutal murder of this young man – did Ian Beggs admit to the world that he was a practising homosexual. It must surely have been a case of the lesser of two evils: admit his true sexuality and ride the storm of humiliation and possible castigation by his family, or face the probability of a trial without a defence.

He had no choice. He had to accept that, at some stage in the future, when he would likely be returned to Scotland for a trial, his secret would be out in the open. In many ways, I believe that he would have feared losing the support of his family, particularly his mother, when the truth was known, much more than facing the prospect of a custodial sentence.

When I spoke to Richard Bache, who had travelled with Beggs to his family home in Ulster and had witnessed the relationship he had with his parents, he, too, was convinced that Beggs was desperate for his mother's approval and feared her recognising the signs of his alternative lifestyle. During that trip home with Bache, which was more or less a flying visit, Beggs had steered his friend away from mentioning anything which could or would raise suspicions about his social life. The family were well known as regular churchgoers and strong advocates of Unionist politics, which were steeped in family values and unambiguous Biblical interpretation. The last thing Beggs wanted to do was to damage the bond he had with the only people who had supported him unconditionally through every one of his previous 'indiscretions'.

It is interesting, when one looks back at the Barry Oldham murder, to see the way in which certain sections of the press almost vilified Oldham, who was the victim, simply because he was known to be a homosexual. Fast-forward 13 years and, incredibly, there were still certain newspapers that could not help but question whether Barry Wallace was himself a homosexual, the implication being that because of a perceived sexuality he may have somehow put himself in harm's way, and have been the architect of his own demise. I can only describe such journalism as salacious and bordering on libellous, but can fully understand why the Wallace family chose not to challenge the comments until the end of the Beggs trial, when their message would be heard loud and clear.

It is hard to imagine just how many man hours are expended

and how much physical work is actually done during a murder investigation unless you are in some way involved. Despite how accurate a TV or film crime drama may seem, it will be an extremely condensed version of events; an hour's worth of entertainment drip-feeding the audience with clue after relevant clue until the suspect is identified and arrested. In the real world, however, there are numerous seemingly mundane tasks which detectives have to carry out as a matter of course which are purely procedural. There are often volumes of witness statements taken which may never be used during the trial, it having been agreed by both the defence and the prosecution that their evidence does not require the appearance of the actual witness in court for purposes of cross-examination.

Each investigation is unique in terms of its circumstances, but the approach to arriving at a case-ready file is invariably the same meticulous process. Every detail of Beggs' movements immediately after the last sighting of Barry Wallace at 1.45 on the morning of 6 December was crucial. There were clues left behind, of course. Beggs may have been clever enough to leave a few red herrings on his way to France, but he could do little about the evidence he had failed to get rid of before his unplanned departure.

It appeared that Ian Beggs had already made a booking at an Edinburgh youth hostel to stay on the night of 5 December. One of the staff at the hostel, Claire Parrott, had been interviewed and recalled that sometime early that evening, Beggs had telephoned to cancel his booking for that night but to confirm a booking for the following night – 6 December. Why had he cancelled? According to Richard Bache, during his telephone conversation with Beggs in the early evening on 5 December, Beggs had said that he was already on the road driving to Edinburgh to stay at the hostel before going to work at Sykes the next day. He had sounded fine but had complained of a cough or a chest infection.

From petrol receipts found in the car he had abandoned at Luton, police had a starting point from which to apply a few tests in relation to the approximate mileage travelled over that two-day period. All sorts of factors had to be applied to the tests, however, including the engine size of the car, its condition and its average miles per gallon. There was no real way of knowing just how much fuel had been left in the tank of the little Peugeot 205 when he purchased fuel on Sunday the 5th, but it could be estimated knowing the capacity of the fuel tank. With that to work from, the receipt from the purchase of fuel on Monday the 6th gave them a stopping point.

It must be accepted that there are variables in this equation, and that there could be several permutations as to what journeys were made during that time. But the figure the police arrived at was at least 100 miles, give or take a few. It was argued that that figure was remarkably close to the return journey from Kilmarnock to Rowardennan at Loch

Lomond. Again, it was not a definitive piece of evidence in the sense of something physical bearing DNA or a fingerprint might have been, but what it helped to do was to support their interpretation of events in relation to the dumping of the remains of Barry Wallace.

The car also had other evidence inside which was much more damning. Traces of blood had been found on the back of the front passenger seat of the vehicle, described as a 'smear', and consistent with something having been squeezed past the seat in order to place it in the rear. The blood was that of Barry Wallace, and the detectives were sure that it had been deposited there as Beggs had loaded the body parts into the car, wrapped up in bags or equivalent wrappings. It seems that Beggs had not been thorough when he had cleaned the car after the event. What he had done, though, was to plan just how he could sanitise the crime scene back at the flat, but again he would need time to do so. He needed a few days to organise things and a few pairs of willing hands to make light of the work. He was going to redecorate.

On Monday, 6 December, Beggs called in sick to work and, although he had made a booking that night at the youth hostel, drove to Edinburgh and stayed at the Hampton Hotel in the city. He did manage to make it in to work the next morning, but didn't stay the full day. Instead, he satisfied his employer that he was genuinely ill, and took the rest of the week as sick leave. He went to his doctor to get a certificate, but, almost immediately after leaving work that Tuesday the

7th, he booked a return trip to Northern Ireland via the Troon ferry, leaving early the next day, with a suggested return date of Sunday, 12 December.

One of his neighbours at Doon Place clearly remembered Beggs – who had been dubbed 'Fred West' by many living in the area who remembered the attack on McQuillan – leaving in a hurry with his car packed right up to window level in the rear passenger area. It was quite possible that somewhere among the items packed away in his car was the severed head of his victim Barry Wallace, and that he had already formulated a plan to throw the head over the side of the boat somewhere between Troon and Belfast harbour.

There is another possibility, of course. Having taken the head with him, intending to bury or dump it somewhere in Northern Ireland where it may never have been found, he may have reconsidered, bearing in mind that there was a chance that his car could be stopped and searched under terrorist legislation at the ferry terminal. At that time in Northern Ireland, stop and search policies were still part and parcel of life, and Beggs may have originally overlooked that very real possibility.

Officers were sent to view any relevant CCTV camera footage which could have shown Beggs boarding and departing the vessel on that date, and any subsequent dates of travel, as it appeared that during that week he returned to Scotland before the weekend and then travelled back to Belfast late that Saturday night.

In between times, receipts found among the many bags of rubbish recovered at Beggs' flat showed that he had visited a B&Q where he had purchased some items with a Switch card bearing the name Forsythe. It would transpire that the card belonged to his aunt, the same one who had acted as 'caretaker' for his flat while he had been in prison during the early Nineties. The CCTV footage showing Beggs in the store had also been found and seized as evidence. The very next day – Saturday, 11 December – he made a trip to Homestyle, where he purchased a roll of wallpaper.

He then returned to Northern Ireland on Saturday evening and, while on board the ferry, sat down to a meal totalling £38.60, the receipt for which was also found at the flat. Documentation found also related to his return trip to Scotland on Sunday, 12 December on the Seacat, which docked at around 6.15 in the evening. For someone who was reported to be sick and too ill to go to work, Beggs had been a busy bee, travelling to and from Ulster twice in the space of four days, and decorating the spare room in the process.

From the search at the flat, it transpired that there was material removed from plastic bin bags which suggested someone had been decorating recently; the smell of paint and paste was still strong even a week later. There had also been a section of carpet cut out and removed from the floor, all relating to the spare room. Why had he only decorated that room? Why not the rest of the flat which he used continually and where there would have been more signs of wear and tear? What had he been trying to hide?

The forensic evidence lifted by the Scene of Crime Officers in attendance was almost overwhelming. There were traces of Barry Wallace's blood on the top of the mattress in the room and on the side as well. There was also blood on the base of the bed, and on the carpet next to where the piece had been cut out. There were traces of blood everywhere in that room, even though Beggs had tried his best to cover it up by staining or painting over it. He wasn't remotely thorough in the job that he had done. If anything, he had been rather blasé. It suggests that in his mind he had not expected the police even to link him to any crime, and he was prepared to do only the bare minimum to clean up after himself.

Already committed to building a solid case against Beggs, the police were given a shocking piece of news from the forensic laboratories, which would stop them in their tracks and make them take stock. There had been numerous blood samples lifted for comparison, and, along with those belonging to Barry Wallace, police were now told that there were as many as a dozen other samples relating to unknown individuals.

The enormity of the situation was clear. It had been suggested before that Beggs was a serial killer, but to date there had been no real evidence to corroborate that theory. Now, however, they were facing the possibility of having to try to identify other victims whose bodies may not yet have surfaced, or had been found in suspicious circumstances and not linked to Beggs. Effectively, it was too much of an investigation for the team to consider expanding its remit until they had dealt with the one case in hand, which was, for want of a better term, 'live'.

One thing they could do, however, in order to eliminate one person, was to make contact with Brian McQuillan, whom they knew to have been attacked in the same room as Wallace, and get a sample of his DNA for comparison.

It was natural for Brian McQuillan to be hesitant about becoming involved with anything regarding Ian Beggs. He had hoped that any association he had had with the man had ended after Beggs' appeal against conviction for the attack on him had been thrown out years before. But in a way he was curious, and echoes of the prediction he had made kept coming back to haunt him. It was as if he had been waiting for the telephone call to tell him that Beggs had done it again. It wasn't a case of 'I told you so', but rather a question of why no one had listened and why the authorities had let this happen.

When contacted by Strathclyde Police, McQuillan was very vocal, telling them that he had a fair idea how Beggs had carried out the attack on Wallace. He described how he had probably singled the young man out as he walked the streets alone in the early hours, possibly drunk and vulnerable, inviting him back to his flat with the promise of more drink. None of this information was in the public domain at the time, and must have been unsettling for Detective Constable Kevin McQueen, who spoke with Brian McQuillan and reached an agreement to take a sample of his DNA.

On the first visit from police, though, McQuillan had the distinct feeling that his outburst, perhaps because of its accuracy, had placed him in a position of suspicion. He was asked questions which could have been put to a potential suspect rather than a person voluntarily assisting police in their enquiries. It was bizarre to say the least. There could never have been a more unlikely pairing, Beggs and one of his previous victims being implicated in a brutal murder as co-accused. If it hadn't been such a serious matter, Brian McQuillan may even have found it funny.

As it was, though, the DNA sample which he provided, and which, according to Detective Superintendent Stephen Heath, would be destroyed after police had made their comparison, was found not to be among the numerous samples lifted from the flat.

That fact alone was even more unsettling for Superintendent Stephen Heath, who had taken over as the Senior Investigating Officer just four months into the case. He would later admit to the press that they had seriously underestimated what they would eventually find at the flat. In comments to the *Sunday Mail*, he said, 'The forensic results were beyond anything we had imagined. A huge amount of blood had been spilled at the flat. Most of it was Barry's, but blood from 17 other people was also found.'

It was a staggering revelation for all involved. They needed to take time to consider how best to preserve evidence now that they had unlimited access to Doon Place and were already collecting items relating to Barry's murder. They now had to take into account that other items could quite possibly be relevant to over a dozen other crimes. From what should have been a reasonably simple search, albeit with numerous pieces of evidence relating to Barry's murder to bag and tag, it turned into a tedious and protracted operation with police teams removing literally thousands of exhibits. It has been suggested that the figure was anywhere between 2,000 and 5,500 items in all.

Included in the recovered items were the personal details of scores of young men, many of whom were foreign students or backpackers who, one way or another, had ended up in Beggs' flat. Photographs and telephone numbers were recovered from drawers and cupboards all over the property and, in one case, even the address and contact number for then Glasgow MP George Galloway was discovered. How he actually managed to obtain that particular detail is a complete mystery. One thing that seems clear is that Beggs had been a hoarder, holding on to little items or 'trophies' left behind by his many unsuspecting visitors. It was crucial that nothing whatsoever was ignored, lest they miss identifying a victim of serious assault or worse.

It must have been impossible not to become a little distracted by the mountains of information in front of them, but the investigation team simply had to deal with the matters at hand. They had a suspect in custody, regardless of the fact that he was still in the Netherlands, for a crime for which the evidence against him was accumulating on an almost daily basis. Making sure they had a watertight case against Beggs, which would secure his incarceration, was the only way they would eventually be able to turn their attention towards widening the scope of their enquiries.

When details of the unidentified blood samples reached the press, they began to speculate about whom the victims may have been, and frantic relatives of missing persons began phoning police involved in the inquiry, demanding they look into the circumstances surrounding the disappearance or death of their loved ones. In light of the response, a decision was made to redeploy some officers from the main investigation in order to take calls and record any details that may identify any more potential victims of Beggs' dubious hospitality.

The three most damning pieces of evidence to be recovered from the flat at Doon Place were a kitchen knife with a serrated edge, a syringe and a handcuff key. The knife itself was probably one which Beggs had used for cutting bread in the kitchen, not something which he had intentionally purchased to serve any other purpose. It was simply a black-handled, everyday kitchen knife. But the amount of blood found in the joint where the blade meets the handle itself made it clear that it had been used for another purpose altogether. It was Barry Wallace's blood congealed in that part of the knife, and the serrated blade was consistent with some of the marks on the bones of his legs and arms, which had been severed. Yet again, Beggs had made a vain attempt at cleaning a vital piece of evidence, instead of actually disposing of it.

The little key found in the flat was instantly recognisable to a police officer as being a handcuff key, although, thorough as they were, the detectives sought the expert opinion of a handcuff manufacturer to give evidence as to what type of key it was and for what purpose it would be used. It was accepted that any defence counsel would argue that the key could have many purposes, but couldn't deny that its primary purpose was to lock and unlock handcuff restraints. It wasn't an offence to possess a set of handcuffs, of course, but considering Barry Wallace had been restrained with cuffs during his assault, it would show that Beggs probably had access to and possession of such an item.

The needle or syringe found was self-explanatory. Granted, when examined, there was no sign of any drug or substance inside the barrel. But it was more than likely Beggs had stuck the needle into the arm of his victim in a further attempt to torture him during his ordeal. When put in that context, the needle was a particularly cruel and wicked twist to events. Imagine the panic of being bound and possibly gagged, having been brutally raped and unable to resist as your attacker presents a syringe filled with clear liquid and injects you in the arm. Imagine that, and you can understand just how Barry Wallace may have died from heart failure.

13

Missing Links

The very simple answer as to why some serial killers remain active and undetected for long periods of time relates to how and where they dispose of their victims. If there are no bodies turning up, then there are no murders to investigate, only missing persons reports at best. With Nilsen, Gacy and Dahmer, there were differing reasons for disposing of the bodies as they did but, in each case, they did not appear to be fazed by either dismemberment or decomposition. The victim of their murderous intent, when finished with, was nothing more than an inconvenience, a matter to be dealt with by whatever means was at hand.

As far as Ian Beggs is concerned, if we look at the Barry Oldham murder first, pathologist Dr Michael Green was of the opinion that there had been an unsuccessful attempt made to dismember the body. Was it just that Beggs had decided it was too impractical to cut up his victim successfully in his flat? There surely would have been some effort involved and probably a lot of disturbance, drawing unwanted attention from others living in rooms in the same house. Or had he been too squeamish to do so?

I would suggest the former, as we already know that part of Beggs' fascination is to cut people and watch them bleed. I don't believe that he necessarily needs to see the effects of the cutting in the sense of the victim's pain. If he did, then drugging or rendering them intoxicated before he inflicts the wounds would deny him that pleasure. In fact, all of the non-mortal wounds found on Oldham's body, which had been described as being 'in symmetrical groups', were delivered post mortem. For him, slicing open the flesh of his victim is deliberate, precise and almost ritualistic. To then dismember the body could be a progression of that behaviour, or simply a means to an end to dispose of it. Whatever the case, I believe Beggs would have been more fascinated than repulsed.

If we then look at the murder of Barry Wallace, it is immediately clear that Beggs the serial killer had reached a point where he found it impossible to control his urges. Regardless of whether it was his intention to kill Barry Wallace from the outset, he was certainly reckless to the point that he could cause his death through positional asphyxiation or shock. Yet he was content to carry out the attack in his flat, the same flat that had already been the scene of a violent crime and a police investigation.

Knowing full well that local police knew what he was capable of, Beggs could not have failed to realise that, should a violent crime such as a razor attack or something similar on a young man occur, detectives would be sure to beat a path to his front door. Was it that he just could not control himself in the heat of the moment? Or was it arrogance? Those obvious risks may, of course, have added to the thrill of the whole experience; the possibility of being caught during or after the event heightening the intensity of the pleasure.

With regard to dismembering the victim's body, we can make the same assumption that was made in relation to Oldham's murder, in that it was more practical to do so in order to move the remains. Crucially, though, the question has to be asked as to why Beggs decided to hold on to the head and dispose of it later, rather than choosing simply to dump it in a different part of the loch at the same time as the other body parts. Was his first intention to keep the head as a trophy? Admittedly, being somewhat forensically aware, Beggs would have realised that dental records would have provided the best tool for identifying the remains, although fingerprints and comparative DNA from the remaining parts of the cadaver could prove just as useful when cross-referenced with any missing persons reports. It was more likely, too, that the head would reappear at some stage considering the way he had casually thrown it from the ferry. Were it not for the police diving team choosing to train at the exact spot where he had thrown the bags into the water, the other body parts might have remained undiscovered there for some time, if not for ever.

Another explanation is that Beggs may have actually wanted the head to be found. Like other prolific killers, Beggs may have wanted to leave a significant item for police to find and then to sit back and watch how the investigation progressed. His feeling of superiority helped further to empower him as a killer, and the longer it took the police to piece things together, the greater that feeling would grow. Only Beggs knows why he kept the head separate from the rest of Barry Wallace's remains, but it had the effect of turning a killer into a crazed monster in the eyes of the general public.

Another question then comes to mind: why did Beggs wait six years after being released from prison to attack his next victim? Perhaps the more appropriate question to ask is whether Beggs did actually wait that length of time to kill again. His other victims' remains may simply not have been discovered or, if they had been, their murders had not yet been linked to Beggs. Those who have dealt with Beggs are convinced that he is responsible for more than the two murders for which he was convicted.

In the words of Detective Chief Superintendent Tony Fitzgerald, the policeman who had led the investigation into the murder of Barry Oldham, on hearing about Beggs' conviction for killing Wallace, 'Beggs being released [after appeal in 1990 for Oldham's murder] was one of the most perverse decisions I've ever come across. He admitted killing this fellow and when it was overturned I was as aghast as everybody else. We believed we were looking for a very dangerous man who may have killed before and could kill again. We felt we were dealing with the beginnings of a serial attacker, a man we needed to get behind bars. What has happened since has proved me right.'

There were three cases in particular which police in Scotland had to consider as being similar enough in circumstance and geography to warrant investigation from the viewpoint of Beggs as a suspect. The family of Glaswegian man Derek Sheerin, in particular his twin sister Diane, were keen to find out if his murder had any links with the 'monster' they had been reading about in the paper.

It was sometime after the weekend of 25 September 1994 when Derek had disappeared, only for his half-naked body to turn up a few days later in undergrowth beside the Celtic Supporters Association in London Road in the city. He had been strangled. According to detectives involved in the original investigation, there had been 'strong homosexual overtones' to the crime, but no serious suspects. Unfortunately for Sheerin's family, police could not prove any involvement by Beggs, and the crime remains unsolved.

Another name put forward as a potential victim of Beggs

was Paul Thomas Christie, a gifted student studying for his Master's degree in environmental studies, who had gone missing in February 1998 from his home in Largs on the west coast of Scotland. By chance, a bone fragment was found in April 2000 by a frogman diving in Largs harbour and, after police divers were called in and scoured the seabed, five more fragments were recovered, along with a boot. The bones had lain on the bottom about 200 yards from the shore, and tests were carried out to establish whether they belonged to Paul. Unfortunately, Paul's mother Christine had passed away in November 1999 after a long illness, never knowing whether he was alive or dead, and it was left to her estranged husband Sandy, Paul's father, to provide a DNA sample from which police were able to confirm a match.

There were elements of the story which mirrored events in the Wallace case, but forensic examination of the bones didn't reveal much in the way of a suggestion of foul play. It may simply have been a case of Paul accidentally falling into the water and getting into difficulties very quickly in the cold February temperatures, and subsequently drowning. But that didn't explain why there had only been a small amount of his skeleton recovered. Where was the rest? It is possible that, after almost two years in the water, and with decomposition taking place fairly rapidly, the flesh and muscle connecting those bones to the skeletal structure, and to each other, would have disappeared, and the ebb and flow of the tides then scattered the pieces of bone far and wide.

Like the Wallace case, where even after a fairly short time immersed in water it was difficult to pinpoint the cause of death, without more substantial parts of Paul Christie's remains to examine, particularly soft tissue fragments, it would be almost impossible to determine how he died or whether it was indeed in suspicious circumstances. To date, there has been no real connection made between Beggs and Christie.

Perhaps one of the cases which most Glaswegians would remember best was that of Colin Swiatek, a 20-year-old with a first-class honours degree in chemical engineering from Strathclyde University, who vanished after a night out on 23 November 1997. His own mother, Norma Swiatek, who lived with her husband Bill in Girvan, described her son as unremarkable, in the sense that she understood why no one had come forward with solid sightings of him after one o'clock on the morning of the 24th, saying, 'I have decided that half the population of Glasgow are boys in their twenties, about 6ft with brown hair, wearing jeans.'

Quite literally, he had disappeared off the face of the earth without a trace, and the search for clues to his whereabouts continued for over a month.

What drew the attention of the police investigating the Wallace murder and charged with following up on other potential victims was the fact that on the night in question when he had gone missing, he had spent the last hour or so in Bennets nightclub. It could have been coincidence, of course, but one they couldn't ignore. Colin had left the club alone and was captured on two separate CCTV cameras walking through the city streets in the opposite direction to where his flat was located in the St Georges Cross area, the perfect target for someone like Beggs – an opportunist who trawled the streets looking for someone on his own.

It was known that Colin had taken two of his bank cards with him that evening in case he needed to withdraw some cash, but, since the last sighting, neither card had been used. If there had been a robbery and Colin had been lying injured or hurt unable to raise an alarm, then it stood to reason that his attackers would have made an attempt to use the cards. On the other hand, if Colin had chosen to run off somewhere of his own free will, then he, too, would have needed to withdraw cash after a day or two, and he clearly hadn't done so. Neither scenario seemed likely.

Some months later, Colin's body was found beneath the waters in the River Clyde, the cause of death determined to be drowning. Understandably frustrating for all involved, the circumstances still remained rather sketchy, with foul play not totally ruled out. But the possibilities of an involvement by Beggs were still not dismissed. To date, the case remains unsolved.

Knowing how Ian Beggs was fond of travelling at home and abroad, the opportunities for him to have committed crimes in numerous other jurisdictions were many and, interestingly, even the Metropolitan Police themselves had set their sights on interviewing Beggs in connection with one unsolved crime committed in the city of London. In December 1998, the head and torso of an unidentified male, described only as 'of Mediterranean origin', were washed up on the banks of the Thames near Deptford in the south-east of the capital. Even though there had been a reward of £5,000 posted for any information which would assist the police in tracking down and prosecuting the person or persons responsible for the murder, the phone lines had been surprisingly silent.

It was a long shot to consider Beggs a strong suspect, with the Met actually admitting as much, even though he may very well have been in London around the time of the discovery of the remains. He was, in truth, only one of a small number of suspects thought to be capable of carrying out such a crime, as dismemberment was recognised as particularly rare for even the most hardened thugs, and that alone was why the detectives waited patiently until any proceedings in Scotland were wrapped up before moving towards speaking to him.

As well as the Met, other constabularies were now considering Beggs as a possible suspect in unsolved crimes in their areas involving similar sets of circumstances. In the north of England, the team investigating the case of 42-year-old lorry driver Bruce Gapper, who had gone missing in Yorkshire after a night out in 1999, saw similarities in the fact that Gapper had been drinking before he literally vanished off the face of the Earth.

As far away as the Isle of Wight, where 16-year-old Damien Nettles was last seen by friends at the end of a night out in 1996, police were willing to consider that Beggs may have featured in some way.

Of course, when someone like Ian Beggs comes to police attention in such a spectacular fashion, then what is known of his modus operandi will be compared against circumstances in other crimes and subjected to further scrutiny. It certainly wasn't a stretch of the imagination to place Beggs anywhere in the country throughout the middle to late Nineties, or to deem him capable of randomly choosing victims for attack.

The details of conversations between Richard Bache and Ian Beggs, as recounted by Bache in the many handwritten notes he made over the time he assisted police in the investigation, held many clues to just how prolific a sex life Beggs may have had, and how he had developed a habit for picking up strays and hitchhikers.

Over meals out in various locations, Beggs would tell his friend Richard about the young men he had met and how he had either taken them back to his flat, or gone to theirs, where they had had sex. On one occasion, during the late spring or early summer of 1999, Beggs had told how he had been approached by a drunk man in George Square in Glasgow who had asked him if he knew where he could get a prostitute. Instead of pointing him in the right direction, Beggs told Bache that he had taken the man back to his flat in Kilmarnock where he had had sex with him. It is a disturbing story, knowing what

we know now about Beggs, and Richard Bache cannot shed
any more light on whether this man had been looking for a
male or female prostitute, or whether the sex, if it took place at
all, was consensual.

According to Bache, Beggs was apparently full of stories
about young men he had met while driving to and from
Edinburgh – hitchhikers he picked up at the side of the road.
They were 'jolly' tales apparently, with no hint of menace.
But in Beggs' world, they, too, could have been stories about
one or more of his victims. From the telephone conversations
in and around the time of the Wallace murder, it is clear that
his best friend did not detect any signs of stress or upset in
Beggs' tone or in the content of the conversation. As well as
the one call on Sunday, 5 December, he had spoken to Beggs
on the Monday after the weekend, again on the Friday of
that week, and again on the Tuesday of the following week.
Other than Beggs complaining about having a chest
infection, and having been sent home from work at Sykes
because of his cough, everything was as normal as it could
have been.

It stands to reason then that, whatever violent or depraved
act Beggs may have carried out on some unsuspecting
traveller he had picked up at the side of the road, it would
have been something he would remember fondly. If true,
these were memories he would treasure and, although he
would refer to them innocently in conversation with Bache,
the version of events he would present would probably have

been heavily sanitised. Only Ian Beggs and perhaps his victim would know exactly what had taken place.

While quizzing Richard Bache as to the times and places he could be certain Beggs and he had been together, the police team asked him to hone in on Sundays in particular. When he told me this, I could sense that Richard Bache believed he had imparted information which he thought was of huge importance in the greater scheme of things. He then told me that he had been told by police that Beggs had almost always carried out attacks on Sundays, hence the reason for wanting him to cross-reference his phone bills with corresponding days on the calendar. However, in the two other serious crimes he had been arrested and prosecuted for, and for which there were definitive dates from which to cross-reference, it appears that both days were random: Barry Oldham was attacked and murdered on a Tuesday, and Brian McQuillan was assaulted on a Friday.

It is not clear as to why the investigation team insisted on this, or what they believed the significance of Sundays were, unless, when looking at some of his other 'slashing' offences, they had identified part of his 'signature', that part of his crime or crimes which was unique to him, and which he would have adhered to when identifying a victim and then carrying out the act. Did he wait until the early hours of a Sunday morning to strike?

Another explanation was that the shifts at Sykes, alongside his commitments to Paisley University, had left Beggs with very small windows during which it may have been possible to carry out crimes such as that of the Wallace murder. Any absenteeism from work would have been well documented, and Sundays may have been the only free days Beggs would have had in which to go hunting. If this were true, then it could help eliminate other possible victims from the inquiry, bearing in mind the need to prove that Beggs had had the opportunity in each and every instance.

I fully understand why Richard Bache was convinced that singling out Sundays as being of importance held more sinister connotations. He was undoubtedly traumatised on learning the truth about Ian Beggs; in some ways, he had been deceived more than anyone else by this person he had thought of as a friend. The man police were describing to him wasn't or couldn't have been a normal human being in any respect. A perfect explanation was that he was a monster; an abomination who chose to kill specifically on the Sabbath day as the ultimate gesture aimed at the suffocating constraints of his religious upbringing. An ordered and logical mind such as that of Richard Bache will undoubtedly dwell upon and continually try to rationalise matters. How better to rationalise the actions of a killer than to believe him irrational?

But it was Beggs' actions after he had been arrested in the Netherlands which helped cement in Richard Bache's mind the fact that he was either unhinged or totally detached from reality. On New Year's morning sometime around 11.00am, while Bache was still in bed suffering from a hangover, he was awoken by a telephone call. To his horror, it was Ian Beggs phoning from jail in Amsterdam, telling him that he was returning his call from two weeks earlier, and asking what he wanted. As Bache remembered, Beggs sounded normal but possibly a little impatient. It was as if he was rather busy, and a tad peeved at having to take time out in order to call him back. The telephone call was extremely unsettling for Richard Bache, and certainly contributed to knocking his confidence.

Then there was the Christmas card Beggs had sent to staff at the university, again while all the drama was unfolding, bearing a simple 'Season's Greeting' with a line in Beggs' own handwriting: 'To all concerned'. This was not normal behaviour at all. Was it just a case of Beggs' taunting and playing mind games with the people around him?

As Bache had continually pointed out to police, during their friendship he and Beggs had never really made small-talk. Their discussions were many and often, but of some substance – debates on morality, social organisation, politics and the nature of reality. Even though Beggs insisted that he did not believe in an objective reality, that things existed only in as far as we perceived them, with each individual creating their own reality, he accepted that there was an 'all-knowing God'. It was Bache who pointed out the inconsistency to him, but all Beggs could offer was that there was an argument which would reconcile the two views. He didn't elaborate. Of course, if Beggs was living in his own reality as such, then what happened in his world was only real to him and him alone; right and wrong was of his own making.

This is how Beggs continually presented himself – as an intellectual who thought deeply about the world around him, presenting alternative yet compelling arguments for differing concepts. He wanted to be seen as the free thinker who questioned what most considered the normal order of things. Interestingly, though, he could never bring himself to deny that one most questionable and least logical of all concepts, the existence of God.

Perhaps it was the manner in which he was brought up as a child; Sunday School and regular worship were part and parcel of the week's activities. Sermon after sermon, hammering on about God the merciful, God the forgiving, God the all-knowing. He rejected scientific thought, calling himself a 'post-modernist'. In his opinion, scientific progress caused more problems than it solved. This from a man working in an IT environment with a background in computer science.

If ever there was a contradiction, then Ian Beggs was it. Even if one were to look back at his first real political affiliation with Ian Paisley's DUP and that leader's denouncement of the Catholic Church and its figure head (the Pope) as being the anti-Christ, one would assume that Beggs would abhor all things Catholic. However, according to Bache, Ian Beggs had told him how his family had developed a relationship with two nuns, described as sisters of Saint Joseph, who were frequent visitors to the Beggs family's home in Ulster. He was quite protective of these women, who he said had carried out some valued work within the prison system, further recalling how one of them had undergone quite an awful ordeal whereby she had been held against her will by an inmate who had subsequently masturbated over her. Without corroboration, of course, it remains a story at best, but there may be a ring of truth to it in the sense that Beggs may have met such persons in his time in prison either in Scotland or England, voluntary prison visitors, perhaps.

At the risk of sounding cynical, one could interpret the respect Beggs maintains for God and all things religious as him hedging his bets. As far as he is concerned, in life, among men, he has no acceptance of judgement by his peers. He refuses to accept any sentencing in a court of law, and has yet to show remorse for his actions. But judgement in the afterlife is another thing altogether. There will be no appeal process to his 'all-knowing God'.

14
Tried and Tested

From the first extradition application made by police in Scotland on 29 December 1999, to the day Ian Beggs stepped off a chartered flight on to Scottish soil to stand trial for murdering Barry Wallace, over a year would elapse. But in all that time, few had forgotten the horrible events surrounding the little flat in Kilmarnock, and the hunt for the 'monster' who had essentially become a household name in Scotland. Even now, some ten years or so later, when the headline 'LIMBS IN THE LOCH MURDER' is printed, most will remember the horrific details of the crime, and many will know Beggs as the killer.

The interest the media had in the case from the outset, particularly their focus on investigating the background of the prime suspect, was what Ian Beggs and his legal team used when fighting extradition in the Dutch courts. His objections to being sent back to Scotland to face charges were not so much based on his innocence, but on the fact that they believed it was unlikely he would receive a fair trial because of his vilification by the press.

The Dutch legal system is renowned for being thorough in affording the subject of an extradition order every opportunity to appeal against a ruling, eventually exhausting every possible avenue. Throughout that year, when one particular court decided on granting the application, Beggs' legal team would appeal against the judgment, hoping the ruling would be overturned. If upheld, they would simply appeal again to a higher court. In November 2000, the Dutch Justice Minister at the time, Benk Korthals, upheld the decision made by the Supreme Court of the Netherlands to send Ian Beggs back to Scotland to face trial. When informed of the decision, the legal team employed by Beggs had seven days in which to launch an appeal through a summary hearing of the same court – the last opportunity they would have to make a case for his remaining in the Netherlands.

For Beggs and his lawyers, the prognosis for the final ruling was not good, bearing in mind that both the panel of judges on the Amsterdam District Court of Justice and on the Supreme Court in The Hague had rejected the notion of a prejudiced trial. When the ruling finally came in January 2001, Ian Beggs was devastated.

As soon as the decision was made on 5 January to hand him over to Scottish police, preparations were being made back in Edinburgh to fend off any possible applications Beggs' legal team in the UK might make in relation to the same argument about negative media coverage. The issue of pre-trial publicity is often a controversial one, and tugs at the very essence of democracy, in that it involves the sanctity of freedom of speech and expression. It is generally accepted that the press play a vital role in both informing and, for that matter, forming public opinion. But with that role comes a responsibility not to interfere with other rights as defined under the Human Rights Act, particularly the right to a fair trial. So-called 'trial by media' can undermine the very aspirations of the general public (those people reading the articles in the first place) in that their wish to have the perpetrator of a crime put behind bars may be frustrated by a successful challenge citing the possibility of an unfair trial.

In general, most newspaper editors are responsible enough to recognise when an article concerning an ongoing case could overstep the mark in terms of prejudicial information, and stop short of printing unfounded rumour and innuendo. In the Beggs case, it was considered that the most damning articles printed were those concerning his alleged expulsion from Northern Ireland at the hands of the paramilitary Ulster Volunteer Force because of his unhealthy sexual interest in young schoolboys. There were, of course, numerous references to his previous convictions for murder and assault, but they would not necessarily have been as emotive as the alleged paedophilia.

The majority of these articles had been printed a full 18 months before the trial was ever to begin, and Lord Coulsfield, presiding over the Appeal Court relating to the application made in Scotland, referred to the time lapse as important in terms of dismissing the appeal. His ruling would most probably have been different had Beggs appeared in court months after the murder had taken place. In fact, he accepted that any judge presiding over such an issue may have had to consider releasing the accused for a period of 12 months or so in order to distance the impact such newspaper articles could have had on potential jurors. Any such decision had to be balanced with the possibility of releasing a dangerous individual back on to the streets, of course, where reoffending would be an even greater issue.

Most court judges, when dealing with an appeal on such grounds, will accept that a trial judge will direct the jury to deal with the facts and the evidence of a case only and to ignore any extraneous material when arriving at a verdict. Whatever manoeuvring Beggs intended to set in motion to counter the overwhelming case against him, blocking the trial because of unfavourable media articles was not one that succeeded.

On 8 January 2001 in the Netherlands, guards approached the cell in which Ian Beggs was being held in order to escort him to Rotterdam Airport, where he was to be handed over to detectives from Scotland for his journey home. What they came across, apparently, was Beggs cowering on the floor covered in his own excrement. According to an article in the *Evening Times*, the guards then had to restrain him physically and hose him down before they could transport him any further. Even when he reached the plane, he refused to walk, and had to be dragged across the tarmac and up the boarding steps by his police escort. His antics didn't end there either, as, when the plane landed, he lay on the floor of the aircraft and had to be dragged along and out to a waiting van, before being driven in a convoy of police cars and motorbikes to Kilmarnock Police Station. According to a source for the *Evening Times*, during each part of the trip, Beggs had supposedly 'cried like a baby'.

His reactions were not what one would have expected from a killer already dubbed a 'beast' and a 'monster', but I suspect it was more born out of frustration than fear. Every aspect of his avoiding custody in late 1999, and his choice of final destination for his flight were deliberate in that he wanted to be able to control what was happening to him and when it would happen. Just as in the attacks on his victims, everything was about how he could control the situation, manipulating and dictating, when possible, every little piece of the scenario. When matters don't quite go his way, then his reaction is one of fury and frustration – a petulant child rolling around on the ground kicking and screaming. It may also be a case of being on the losing side perhaps, something which Beggs was not particularly used to. Other than his appeal against conviction for the attack on Brian McQuillan, Beggs had triumphed in many legal cases, not least his acquittal on appeal for the Barry Oldham murder. Was it simply a case of his being a bad loser?

The fact was that Ian Beggs could see the writing on the wall well before he ever arrived back on Scottish soil. Even without full disclosure of the mountain of evidence accumulated by the police, he would have known that, barring a legal loophole, the case against him was formidable.

On 10 January 2001, William Ian Frederick Beggs was driven to Kilmarnock Sheriff Court in the back of a Renault Espace with blacked-out windows to hear the charges of the abduction and murder of supermarket worker Barry Wallace read to him in open court. Security was fairly tight for his brief appearance, with around 40 police officers on duty around the courthouse. A crowd of around 70 people had gathered for the event and, as expected, Beggs made no plea to the charges.

The Procurator Fiscal John Watt confirmed all details to the waiting press, and stated that an order was also made by the court under the Contempt of Court Act preventing the release of further information. Beggs was committed to Barlinnie Prison in Glasgow where he was to be held pending the outcome of further enquiries.

It would be Tuesday, 18 September 2001 before the

Wallace murder trial began at the High Court in Edinburgh, with the jury of eight men and seven women. The format for a jury in Scotland is somewhat different from the rest of the UK, and not just in terms of its numbers. The theory behind having such a large number is that it brings with it a broad and diverse range of viewpoints and life experiences with which to determine the complex issues presented in any legal case. Even if one or two jurors were to drop out during a trial for one reason or another, matters could continue so long as the total number of remaining jurors does not fall below twelve. The most significant difference, however, comes from the fact that a Scottish jury is able to return a verdict by simple majority – eight jurors need to be in agreement, regardless of whether the jury has been reduced in size to twelve. In certain cases where a verdict has been arrived at with such a narrow majority, it is often cited during arguments in mitigation of a reduced sentence, although not necessarily successfully.

The male and female jurors selected for the Beggs trial would have had to have included patience among their many attributes, as from the outset it was clear that there would be many disruptions brought about by Beggs' defence counsel led by Donald Findlay QC, a formidable court performer with an uncompromising cross-examination technique. On day two of the trial, presiding judge Lord Osborne excluded the jury from court for two hours in order to hear a debate on a legal matter, the nature of which would not be revealed by the press due to reporting restrictions. It was clear, however, that, whatever the issue was, its complexity required further investigation and discussion, with an eventual decision to be made by Lord Osborne. In light of this, he sent the jury home for two days, to return on Friday at the end of the first week.

This interruption was to be one of many throughout the trial, each one an attempt by the defence to have one piece of evidence or another excluded from being heard by the jury in open court. Most, if not all, of the objections raised had been done so by Beggs himself, who had continually prompted his counsel to take issue and seek ruling from the trial judge. It must have been frustrating for Donald Findlay QC to try to construct a plausible defence and gain the jury's sympathy for his client, when to everyone it seemed that each delay was nothing more than an elaborate smokescreen. The jury would never have been privy to the content of the legal arguments thrashed out in their absence, but they were in no doubt as to who had raised the objections in the first place.

The choice of Donald Findlay as Beggs' counsel is interesting in itself; both men shared an interest in Conservative politics as well as Unionism in Scotland and Northern Ireland. Findlay held the post of vice-chairman of Rangers Football Club, historically a Protestant club, with strong sectarian elements within the membership and fans.

To anyone casting an eye over the disclosure schedules –

information released by the prosecution to the counsel acting on behalf of Beggs, outlining the strength of their case and the evidence available – it would have been clear that the odds had been stacked in favour of the prosecution. Those odds were even shorter when it transpired that the man chosen to be prosecuting counsel was Alan Turnbull QC. It was Turnbull who had been one of the two prosecutors during the trial of the Pan Am flight 103 Lockerbie bomber Abdelbaset Ali Mohmed al-Megrahi. Considering the huge scale of the Lockerbie investigation and the impact and interest it had worldwide, it was no surprise that the trial itself was covered by virtually every news network around the globe.

Rather than be overwhelmed by performing on such a grand scale, Turnbull was in his element. Throughout that trial, it was apparent that al-Megrahi would not be giving evidence in the box, and Turnbull made sure that he took every opportunity to turn that to his advantage.

In some ways, the Lockerbie trial and that of Beggs' would be similar in that, from the outset, both legal teams would have recognised what a mistake it would be for Ian Beggs to take the stand. What Alan Turnbull wanted was to exploit that weakness, to goad Beggs into changing the game plan, and to get an opportunity to cross-examine him in the witness box where he was sure Beggs' arrogance would resonate through the jury and the courtroom in general.

For Donald Findlay and the team defending Beggs, there

were few opportunities to score points during cross-examination of the several witnesses called to give evidence against Beggs. When faced with the compelling story that had been provided by Kenneth Petrie, who had sadly died before the matter came to court, but whose testimony had been allowed to be heard in the form of his statement read out by Detective Constable Robertson, Findlay had little choice but to suggest to the jury that the statement could have been given by a disgruntled Petrie – a man with an axe to grind for some reason known only to himself. He also pointed out that Petrie may not have been exactly comfortable being spoken to by detectives, and may have said anything in order to get out of the police station quickly that afternoon. Of course, neither he nor the jury would ever have the opportunity to ask Mr Petrie himself, and Findlay was at pains to point that out, as well as how they all had to rely on Detective Constable Robertson's summary of events from which to make up their minds.

What the jury were left with was the content of conversations between the two men, when Ian Beggs had told Petrie how he liked to trawl the streets in the early hours looking for men to pick up, straight or gay, and how he often enjoyed the challenge of picking up straight men in straight bars. It was hard to cast doubt on those statements unless Beggs himself took the stand.

The tactic of attempting to cast doubt and undermine testimony given by prosecution witnesses is fairly standard practice, of course, but without a solid alibi or questionable forensics with which to argue someone's innocence, it is nothing more than an exercise in trying to put out fires. When a jury hears emotive evidence such as that given by Richard Bache, and it is placed in context for them by an experienced prosecutor like Alan Turnbull, it can almost outweigh the most damning of physical evidence. That ten-minute telephone call between Bache and Beggs on Sunday, 5 December in the early evening, when Richard Bache said that Ian Beggs had told him of having met a 'sweet' or 'cute' young man, was possibly the most disturbing mental image the jury were subjected to. The court had already been told that, as the two men spoke, it was likely that the remains of Barry Wallace were somewhere in the rear of that car wrapped in bin bags, while Ian Beggs drove along the picturesque, twisting roads leading towards Balmaha pier. The almost innocuous nature of the conversation, but in particular Beggs' seemingly unaffected 'smug' attitude when describing his sexual conquest of the night before, all taking place amid the blood and gore of a young man's dismembered body, conjured up an image of a ruthless, detached killer. How then to counter such evidence?

When Donald Findlay cross-examined Richard Bache, it was directed specifically at the choice of words Bache had claimed Ian Beggs had used to describe the young man he had met on 5 December 1999. After a little badgering, Bache accepted that Beggs may not have used those exact words, but something similar, saying, 'I don't remember his precise words but the essence of it was as I have put in my own words. That's probably a fairly fair description of it, yes.'

Regardless of the issues Richard Bache had been struggling to come to terms with – anxiety and depression, among other things, all of which were symptoms of post-traumatic stress – he was proving to be a formidable presence in the witness box. When Donald Findlay homed in on the content of the first statement Bache had supplied to police on 20 December 1999, just two weeks after the murder had taken place, and pointed out the obvious omission of the details of the call on 5 December, Richard Bache could only explain that he had been deeply traumatised at learning about what had happened, and had been prescribed anti-depressants by his GP. Again, Findlay probed as to when exactly he had told detectives about the call and Beggs' boast of his sexual conquest. It may have worried Alan Turnbull somewhat that the impact of Bache's story was being diluted, but he held back with any objection.

Although under a great deal of pressure from Findlay, Richard Bache remained focused and explained that he had only remembered the content of the telephone call as it had come back to him in a flashback, and that it had been sometime in January 2000 when he had made a further statement to police. He even admitted to the court that at first he had doubted what he remembered, but because it was in context with something else – a mention by Beggs that he was suffering from bronchitis or a chest infection – he was able to 'cross-reference' the two memories and realise that it was indeed what had happened.

Unless you actually know or have met and conversed with Richard Bache, his explanation may have seemed extraordinary. The way in which Richard processes information may not be what many of us do ourselves, but he is by no means alone in that. He has an extremely ordered mind – logical and analytical – drawing conclusions only after gathering and collating all the relevant information at his disposal.

It was clear that Findlay was not at all convinced, but he hadn't shaken Bache. Findlay fixed him with a stare. 'And are these ladies and gentlemen of the jury to take it, Mr Bache, that you are being serious about asking them to believe this nonsense?'

When Richard Bache replied, it was heartfelt. 'I wish … I hope they do believe it, yes, and it is not nonsense.'

While this piece of evidence was particularly damning for Beggs, Findlay drew the line at overstating his case that Richard Bache had invented the content of the telephone conversation. There was, of course, no doubt that it had taken place – telephone records would prove that – but he, too, knew that there were only two people who could really know what had been said.

Findlay's sparring partner, Alan Turnbull, was on his feet

almost immediately to re-examine Bache and was at pains to point out that very same fact. In effect, he was highlighting the fact that Beggs himself, being the other party in the conversation, was not willing to stand in the box and give his own account of what had happened. Why, if Findlay thought Richard Bache had lied about the 'sweet young man' comment, did he not call the most obvious witness to counter that statement?

The other issues that Findlay raised with Bache were the idea that Ian Beggs had been familiar with the area around Loch Lomond, and whether it was possible that gay men sometimes sought out other gay men in straight pubs. Again, in terms of real evidence, the fact that Loch Lomond was a tourist area known and frequented by many people was neither here nor there. Yes, Bache could say that Ian Beggs had taken some friends from Northern Ireland there to stay at a youth hostel, and that it had been a natural choice because of its picturesque beauty, and that Beggs had actually pointed out the road to Balmaha pier to him on one occasion, saying that the road 'went nowhere – it was a dead end'. No one had argued that it would have taken someone with a unique knowledge of the area to be able to navigate their way to Balmaha pier that day to dump the body parts. Nor had anyone suggested that Beggs had some sort of connection with the loch in terms of its being his 'favourite' place. The relevance of that thread of questioning was lost on many.

However, the questions relating to gay men and straight bars hit upon an area which would prove to be a high-risk strategy for Donald Findlay. There was no subtlety when Findlay attempted to portray the victim, Barry Wallace, as a homosexual, fully compliant in a consensual sexual act in the early hours of the morning of 5 December 1999. While caught up in the act, according to Findlay, Wallace had unfortunately choked and died. Faced with the horror of this young man dead in his flat, Beggs had panicked and had done what he had in order to clear up what Findlay suggested was an awful mistake.

This was something which I suspect Donald Findlay would not have been all that comfortable with, but may have been pushed into running with by his client. Those who knew the background of Ian Beggs would, of course, remember that he had claimed before that the death of Barry Oldham had also been a horrible mistake. Without fear of reproach, Donald Findlay would defend a client by any means, and was purported to have said that he believed that there was no such thing as a lost cause. But surely this was something else. The Wallace family should never have been subjected to the harrowing experience of a trial, let alone having to listen to the memory of their son being tarnished by unfounded innuendo.

On 10 October, Alan Turnbull rose to address the court in his closing submissions. For many of the jury, it was the time that each single strand of evidence, which had been presented to them during the days of the trial, would be woven together to form the basis of an interpretation of events over the weekend of 4–6 December 1999, when a young man had died a horrible death. There were, of course, those jurors who had already formed an opinion as to the relevance of each exhibit or significant statement and, for them, it would either be an affirmation of what they already knew or a challenge to their perception.

When Turnbull began by pointing out that the case was circumstantial, he referred to the fact that there were no witnesses who had actually seen Mr Beggs murder Barry Wallace, rather that there was a combination of different circumstances. These 'circumstances', he continued, were often a number of different facts, which, if examined in isolation without looking at them against other facts in the case, could possibly be explained away fairly easily. However, when all of the facts were taken together, he then explained, 'the power of their combination becomes clear'.

Without charging straight in, linking the evidence together to form the basis of the bigger picture, he started by addressing the single pieces of circumstantial evidence on their own and conceded that, if they were looked upon as such individually, there may be other rational explanations. He first commented on the blood found in Beggs' flat that was determined to be that of Barry Wallace, and agreed that it didn't necessarily mean that Barry had ever been in the house.

Turning to the handcuff key, he again conceded that, as a stand-alone piece of evidence, it didn't mean that Beggs had owned a set of handcuffs around the time of the murder, let alone applied them to Wallace's wrists and ankles. Again, the discovery of a syringe at the flat at Doon Place could on its own mean absolutely nothing, other than it was found during the search. The anal injuries found on Barry's body, he stated, may have been caused, as Findlay had suggested, by 'rough sex'. Even the decorating of the bedroom, the blood on the knife, the Scandinavian Seaways plastic bags and the fact that Beggs had skipped the country when sought by police, in themselves, taken alone, could be interpreted in a number of ways. Crucially, when all that evidence was brought together, though, Turnbull offered that there could be no other explanation than the fact that William Ian Frederick Beggs had brutally assaulted, murdered and dismembered teenager Barry Wallace.

Dealing first with the blood found in the flat at Doon Place, Turnbull referred to the witness evidence given by Graham Boax and Wesley Kirkland in court, in which it was apparent that, after the scuffle at the taxi rank in the town that evening, Barry had not been bleeding. Reminding the jury of the large quantity of Barry's blood found in Beggs' flat, Turnbull dismissed the explanation that the two men had simply come into contact with each other and that, because Barry had been bleeding, there had been transference from Wallace to Beggs. If it had been simple transference, asked Turnbull, how had the blood found its way on to the door of the washing machine, the top of the mattress in the spare room, alongside the base of the bed, and on to the carpet under the bed adjoining where there was a missing section? In addition, Turnbull asked, how could there have been blood transferred on to the serrated edge of the kitchen knife, particularly at the point where the blade joins the handle? Was it possible? It was extremely unlikely. The blood in the spare room and the blood on the knife offered only one explanation, and that was that Barry Wallace had been in Beggs' flat that evening. And, during the trial, the knife with Barry's blood on it was the only piece of evidence for which Donald Findlay had offered no explanation.

Next, Turnbull turned his attention towards the handcuff key found in the flat, and to the results of the post-mortem performed by Mr Morrison, who stated that injuries caused by handcuffs having been applied to Barry's wrists and ankles had occurred just before his death. Putting these key pieces of evidence together – the blood in the flat, the knife itself and the handcuff key – meant that there was only one plausible explanation and that was that Barry Wallace had been present at the flat before he met his death. If the jury accepted his version of events, then quite simply he had shown that Beggs had the means to commit the murder and, to some degree, the opportunity.

The all-important timeline of events on the evening of 4

December into the early hours of 5 December was then explored. From the evidence given by those at their work's party and in Kilmarnock town centre who had seen Barry, Turnbull said it was clear that Barry Wallace had been 'too drunk to be making sensible decisions'. He reminded the jurors that, according to those witnesses, Barry was last seen at around 1.45am.

Turning to the statements made by Andrew Aird, Beggs' colleague from Sykes who had been at the same party in Edinburgh, he had said that Beggs had left in his car to drive back to Kilmarnock sometime around 12.00–12.30am, certainly no later. Regardless of the variables, which Turnbull admitted there would always be, the journey would have taken around an hour-and-a-half, and would have put Ian Beggs in Kilmarnock town centre at about 2.00 that morning – around the same time Barry had been there.

Again, Turnbull was pressing home the aspect of opportunity, but where would the motive for the crime come from, if indeed there was a motive? Why had Barry been coaxed back to the flat in the first place?

The statement made by Kenneth Petrie to police provided the key to summing up those issues. Turnbull then read extracts from that statement, simple pieces of information which would concentrate the minds of everyone in the court.

'I am gay. I frequent the Edinburgh gay scene. I have been doing so for about three years now. I regularly attend Number

18 Sauna and the New Town Bar. I was in the Number 18 Sauna and the New Town Bar and got to know Ian Beggs. I have known Ian Beggs casually for about two years now. Although I know Ian Beggs has a car, I have never been in his car or seen it. Through talking to him, I know he lives in Kilmarnock.'

There were other less important pieces of information which Turnbull chose to leave out, moving quickly to the relevant paragraphs: 'Ian also discussed with me how he would rather pick up a guy from a straight pub as opposed to from a gay pub. I told him I couldn't do that because I was scared I would get assaulted. Ian said he would befriend them first. He said that some of them had quite a lot of drink in them. He said he would say, "Come back to my flat for more drink." Once they were drunk, he would offer to share a bed with them or tell them they could sleep on the floor. After getting them into bed, Ian didn't specify how he managed to have sex with them but the impression he gave, that is what I suppose happened. Ian said the guys he preferred were younger guys.'

The last important few lines of the statement concluded, 'Ian told me he liked to cruise early morning in an attempt to pick up young guys in his car.'

There it was in black and white. Regardless of the fact that Petrie was not there in person, if his evidence was to be believed, it was as good as hearing an admission from Ian Beggs that he regularly cruised in the early hours of the morning looking for young men, gay or straight, drunk or incapable, whom he then coaxed into going to his flat with the promise of more drink, where he later had sex with them, possibly without their consent. He was a dangerous, calculating, sexual predator. In simple terms, that was his motive, and that was how Barry came to be at Doon Place.

But Petrie's evidence was not stand-alone. Alan Turnbull reminded the jury of the evidence Richard Bache had given, and how, despite what Findlay had said in calling Bache a liar, there had been no contrary evidence offered. In essence, Findlay had expressed an opinion as counsel, but that was all that it was. The facts were that Ian Beggs had recounted to Bache an obvious sexual encounter the previous evening with his 'sweet' or 'cute' young man, and that was in itself consistent with the type of practices Kenneth Petrie had described to police.

In essence, without the testimony of Richard Bache and Kenneth Petrie, all that Ian Beggs was likely to be convicted of was culpable homicide. In answer to the many critics of Richard Bache, both professionally and personally, his evidence was going to be crucial for the prosecution.

There was no doubt that Turnbull had the jury hanging on his every word. He had anticipated any areas where doubt may still have remained, and focused on dealing with and dispelling those doubts, leaving no room for manoeuvre for Findlay. The one simple fact that he knew from the start that many jurors would struggle with was that it had been impossible to determine exactly how Barry Wallace had died. The defence had been at pains to say that it had been an accident, Barry choking or suffocating while taking part in rough consensual sex. Turnbull had already dealt with the consensual sex issue, reminding jurors of the terrible injuries on Barry's wrists and ankles consistent with a very violent struggle, and the injuries to his anus suggesting anything but consensual sex, as well as to the fact that witness evidence had shown that Barry was heterosexual. But what of the cause of death?

He did agree that, during the incident, Barry had died from either heart failure or asphyxia, but what he was clear on and what he wished the jury to also consider was that Beggs had been totally reckless as to the possible consequences of the attack. Cleverly, he set out an example whereby he suggested that, if a woman had died during a rape, possibly asphyxiated as her face was pushed down into a pillow during the assault, then at the very least it would be considered culpable homicide. At worst, taking all the circumstances into consideration, it would be murder. The same applied to the Wallace case. Each and every piece of evidence suggested that Beggs had launched a serious and violent attack on Wallace without thought or concern as to whether he could cause him serious injury or death. Together with the dismemberment of the body, this was clearly a case of murder.

In all, the typed document for Turnbull's closing

submissions covered 46 pages, providing one hour and twenty minutes of an impassioned plea for justice for the Wallace family. The case against Ian Beggs was circumstantial, but Turnbull had added structure and clarity when piecing it together, so that even the most obtuse of jurors would recognise the clear guilt of the accused. It was now left to Donald Findlay to retrieve what he could from the situation.

Findlay told the court that 'there was not a scrap of evidence' that his client was guilty of murder. The closing submission for the defence could only be described as a two-hour-long circuitous journey of innuendo and desperation. Yet again, Findlay suggested that the homosexual element to the crime was what the jury seemed to be concentrating on, and that this in itself could be tainting their opinion. He asked the jury to put aside their prejudices, stating, 'There are undertones in this case. That somehow, if it can be that Mr Beggs is a homosexual, that tells you all you need to know. It is not a crime to be gay, and, if Mr Beggs is gay or not, it is not a crime for him either.'

But he wasn't only referring to Ian Beggs. He was, of course, reminding the jury that, as far as the defence were concerned, Barry had been a willing sexual partner, and that the turn of events thereafter had been nothing more than unfortunate. Pointing out to the court that dismemberment of a body was not in itself an offence under Scottish law, Findlay's final plea to the jury was a hollow one: 'You cannot and must not convict somebody of a crime that has not been proved because you are disgusted by what happened after it. That would not be justice.'

The jury retired.

15

Life for a Life

It took the jury just over two hours of deliberations before informing the clerk that they had reached a verdict. By a majority, William Ian Frederick Beggs was found guilty of murdering Barry Wallace. It was 12 October, 17 days after the trial had begun and over 22 months since Barry's murder. According to eyewitnesses in the courtroom, the usually confident Beggs looked shaken by the decision as he was led down to the court cells to await sentencing.

In other jurisdictions, when a person has been found guilty of a crime, including that of murder, it is usually the case that the sentencing is deferred until pre-sentence reports are prepared in mitigation of a lengthy custodial term being handed out. The defendant is returned some weeks later when the judge will give consideration to all the factors which may or may not affect his decision-making. For instance, an early guilty plea in a case, saving witnesses the stress of appearing in court as well as taxpayers' money, might result in a reduction in terms of prison time. Other mitigating factors might include full and frank co-operation with police during the investigative process, including taking other crimes into consideration (or the TIC process, as it is more commonly known), whereby the accused confesses to other crimes, helping police clear previously unsolved cases. Those other crimes are then dealt with by way of a concurrent custodial sentence.

For Beggs, however, there were no factors which Donald Findlay could cite as being worthy of leniency. He did, however, offer a few words which suggested Beggs had been 'touched' by Barry Wallace's death. He told the court, 'It should not be thought that Mr Beggs is unmoved or unaffected by the events that occurred in December 1999. But to convey that either to the court or indeed anyone else places one in the danger and in the position of saying something that seems to be trite, and therefore I don't.'

If this was an attempt at displaying some sort of remorse on behalf of his client, it indeed fell short. What did have an enormous impact upon the jury, though, was when Alan Turnbull made them aware of Beggs' previous convictions, including the attack on Brian McQuillan in 1991, which had taken place in the very same flat where he had murdered Barry Wallace. If anyone in the jury had held even the slightest doubt about Beggs being guilty of murder, that doubt had now disappeared.

In the cells below the court, Beggs was apparently going berserk. He was reportedly stomping around, pulling at his hair and throwing food at the walls. The scenes were reminiscent of his extradition when he rolled around the floor kicking and screaming. Yet again, Beggs had lost control of the situation.

When Lord Osborne asked for him to be brought back up to the court, it was clear to all that Beggs had been crying. His eyes were red-rimmed, and all colour had drained from his face. Without hesitation, Lord Osborne sentenced him to life in prison, describing the murder of Barry Wallace as an 'appalling' crime, and warranting that a minimum term of at least 20 years be served. But he wasn't finished there, warning Beggs, 'I should make it clear that, at the end of the specified period, you will not necessarily be released on licence. Whether you are will depend on the Parole Board for Scotland determining that it is no longer necessary for the protection of the public that you should continue to be confined to prison.'

He also ordered that Beggs' name be added to the sex offenders' register, only an issue should he ever be released, but a bitter blow to Beggs, bringing even more shame upon his family.

When leaving the dock, Beggs kept his head down and avoided eye contact with anyone in the public gallery. The self-assured and arrogant man who had shown little emotion throughout the trial was deflated and resigned. Within the hour, he was spirited away to Saughton Prison in a closed van, desperately trying to hide his face from the cameras.

There was a great outpouring of emotion from Barry Wallace's family and friends as they left the courtroom after hearing the verdict. Throughout the investigation, but particularly throughout the trial, the Wallace family had listened as their son's reputation had been dragged through the mud by the defence counsel, with every word being reported on and printed in every major newspaper around the country. Up until the sentence had been passed, the family had never uttered a word to the press but, as matters came to a close, Ian Wallace, while holding hands with his wife, Christine, and remaining son, Colin, stood outside the court and read a statement:

> 'Christine, Colin and I would like to take this opportunity to thank our families, friends and Strathclyde Police, particularly our liaison officer Inspector John Miller, for the overwhelming support and comfort we have received during the most tragic period of our lives.
>
> 'We are just a normal family who have sat quietly for 22 months trying to maintain our dignity while our young son's name and reputation has been dragged through the gutter by some aspects of the media. We now think it is the time to put the record straight.

'Anyone who knew Barry would know that he was not an individual who, after having a good night with everyone else at his work's Christmas party, would decide of his own free will to go away with this perverted, murdering homosexual. Our Barry was a normal, healthy, fun-loving teenager whose only mistake in this whole sordid episode was to be in the wrong place at the wrong time and fall prey to this monster, a mistake which cost him his life.'

After thanking the Procurator Fiscal's office and the jury members who sat through such a distressing trial, Ian Wallace concluded that he was glad that Beggs had finally been put behind bars, and that he hoped certain others who had helped Beggs 'cover his tracks' would themselves soon be brought to justice.

It was clear that Ian Wallace was referring to Beggs' parents and his elderly aunt when he spoke of the 'others', and his bitterness was fully understandable, but there were parts of his statement which were uncomfortable for some. No one would argue that Ian Wallace had the right to stand up and defend his son's reputation, if that indeed was what was being questioned. But many were quick to point out that, if it were found to be true that Barry had been a young homosexual male, and his parents had not been aware of it, would that mean that his reputation would have been sullied? Did Ian Wallace believe that gay or lesbian relationships were wrong, and was he being inappropriately vocal about the 'abnormality' of a gay lifestyle?

This stigma which surrounds gay sexual relationships is very much the issue which arguably may have driven Ian Beggs to do what he did to other men. Having already explored his possible motives in this book, it would be pointless to cover that ground again, but the stigma of same-sex relationships had been identified as the reason why some of Beggs' earlier slashing victims had gone underground, unwilling to come forward and testify against him in court. Ironically, had they done so, Beggs may have been incarcerated much sooner, and been entered on to the sex offenders' register, empowering the authorities with all manner of restrictions that could be imposed upon him.

There was no evidence to suggest that Barry was anything other than a young heterosexual male but, if there had been, then one has to ask why it was never presented in court. Ian Wallace was right when he said that his son had been in the wrong place at the wrong time, a victim of circumstance, and that alone.

No one, least of all the Wallace family, expected that this would be the last they would hear of Beggs, but for now the hardest part for them was over.

Meanwhile, the immediate consideration for Donald Findlay and his team would be to launch an appeal against conviction and sentence, and there were issues with which they were unhappy – the very same issues which had stopped proceedings on the second day of the trial, but which could not be reported on at the time or heard by the jury.

At the end of the first day of the trial, Donald Findlay had approached Lord Osborne and presented him with certain material which he said had been downloaded from the Internet that very day and which, in his opinion, would undoubtedly prejudice any jury against his client. The offending article was taken from *Gary Otton's Scottish Media Monitor*, and in parts referred the reader to Beggs' previous offending history and sexual behaviour, paying particular attention to his conviction for murder in England and the subsequent successful appeal. Findlay was calling for the removal of the article from the website and, if that did not happen, then he urged the publishers be brought before the court in contempt.

The response to Findlay's concerns from Alan Turnbull was immediate. When in session the next day, Turnbull pointed out that he agreed that some parts of the material had been 'inappropriate', but he argued that the article had not been contemporaneous, the original date for publication being early 2000. He also stated that he had carried out an Internet search using the name William Beggs, and was satisfied that, initially, the *Scottish Media Monitor* article did not appear among the many other articles about the accused.

Matters did not rest there, however, as Findlay produced numerous other Internet articles from sources such as the *Guardian* newspaper, the *Sunday Times* and the *Sunday Herald*. Each of these articles was less than complimentary about Beggs and, in the case of the *Sunday Times*, he had already been dubbed 'the Gay Ripper'.

It wasn't so much the amount of material as the content. Presenting his case to Lord Osborne, Donald Findlay argued that, in the first instance, his client's previous convictions had been disclosed, including the one which had been quashed on appeal. Second, his client's character had been attacked, and that in itself would never have been an issue in the proceedings. Third, he was concerned as to the sensationalism of some of the reports, one in particular which likened Beggs to Fred West. Fourth, he was convinced that such was the inaccuracy of the reports – in particular relating to the fact that no references to Beggs' character or convictions had been heard during the short period in which the trial had been in session – that it could be considered a contempt of court under the Act. And last, if any of the offending material were to come into the hands of the jury, he considered it would indeed prejudice a decision, and that no amount of direction by the judge could 'cure' that prejudice.

Effectively, this was an argument of its time in the sense that the rules relating to contempt of court had been written with newspapers, books and magazines in mind, and certainly not the Internet. The way in which people sought out news or information was changing radically, and a fundamental change in the Contempt of Court Act may have had to have been considered.

When he returned to court on 20 September, Alan Turnbull outlined his opinion on the matter saying that he believed that the time of the publication of the articles in question predated the trial by some considerable months, and therefore could not be considered contemporaneous. In addition, he argued that viewing an article on a website was just the same as going along to a library and looking through back copies of newspapers. In essence, Turnbull was clear that, in terms of the Act itself, the articles did not create 'a substantial risk that the course of justice in the proceedings in question will be seriously impeded or prejudiced'.

For Donald Findlay, however, matters were not so clear cut, and he argued that the very fact that the articles remained on a website meant that the material was being published there and then. He also reminded Lord Osborne of the sensationalism of the original reporting on the 'limbs in the loch' murder, and did not for one minute believe that jurors who conducted a search on the Internet would not be able to come across such articles.

The trial continued after Lord Osborne agreed with the opinion of the Advocate Depute, in that he believed it was unlikely any juror would be able to easily access the articles in question, and that he had no reason to suppose any jury would ignore the direction of a trial judge, if indeed they had already accessed possible prejudicial material.

In fact, that decision made in the early part of the trial would end up being only one of the nine grounds for an appeal which was lodged on 2 July 2002.

If past experiences were anything to go by, Ian Beggs

would be pursuing his appeal with vigour, and dominating the time of whatever legal team had the misfortune to represent him. The first hurdle that had to be overcome was a sift, carried out by an appeal judge, which would effectively determine whether there were sufficient salient points of law regarding the original trial which were arguable. The decision came in January 2003, with the first-sift judge concluding that up to five of the nine points could be considered specified. Unhappy with that, two months later, in March, Beggs' legal team launched an appeal of the first-sift judge's decision. In August of that year, three second-sift judges refused that appeal on its merits.

In May 2004, Beggs and his legal team lodged their appeal to the High Court complaining about the second-sift judges' decision and, after much deliberation, in November 2005, the Lord Justice General returned the decision to grant leave to appeal.

The mechanics of the law, regardless of whether it is during the prosecution stages of a matter or the appeals process after conviction, are undeniably laborious and frustrating, but there is method in madness. The sift process in any appeal is designed to weed out frivolous grounds which, in turn, may stop any petition in its tracks, and save the matter progressing any further through the system. Decisions at each level require the experience and interpretation of some of the best legal minds in the judiciary, often relying on case law to return a balanced conclusion. Like it or loathe it, in the

United Kingdom every convicted prisoner is afforded the opportunity to exhaust the appeal system and, in virtually every instance, with the assistance of legal aid.

Eventually, in September 2009, Ian Beggs was returned to the same courtroom where he had been tried for the murder of Barry Wallace to start proceedings in his appeal. The greatest emphasis in the appeal was placed on what Beggs' legal counsel described as a 'hostile and speculative press campaign', which in their opinion had not afforded their client a fair trial. Also at issue were arguments attacking the whole extradition process from the Netherlands, which they described as having breached rules, and the fact that they believed the warrant that had been issued to search Beggs' flat at Kilmarnock was invalid. There was more, of course, and each and every point would be lengthy and immersed in almost indecipherable legalese.

These were all very complex issues, and for that reason the appeal panel had to retire at the conclusion of the proceedings and take some time before returning their decision. Almost six months later and in a 128-page document, Lord Eassie, Lady Paton and Lord Bannatyne released their findings, wholly dismissing the appeal and stating that in their opinion none of the grounds of appeal was well founded.

It was finally official. Ian Beggs would remain in prison for the duration of his sentence. Another sigh of relief for the Wallace family and another opportunity for them to move forward with their lives, which had understandably been put on hold through Beggs' continual legal manoeuvring. Despite the odds, Beggs' counsel, on his instructions, made an immediate application to take the matter to the UK Supreme Court based on four separate grounds, but this, too, was rejected less than three months later in May 2010, by the same three senior judges who had sat in consideration of his appeal at the Edinburgh court.

But would this turn out to be the final chapter in the saga of the Ian Beggs story?

16
Rattling the Cage

I was close to finishing this book when it was announced that Ian Beggs had lost his appeal against conviction and sentence, the decision coming almost ten years on from the original trial. It was Richard Bache who broke the news to me by e-mail, and I couldn't help but wonder what Beggs' reaction had been. After so much time, and almost halfway through his minimum term, would he finally accept the Court of Appeal's decision, and admit his guilt to the world? Even though his possible release would undoubtedly be aided by such admissions, along with sincere expressions of remorse, I suspect Beggs will never bring himself to do so.

In April 2010, I wrote Ian Beggs a letter and sent it to Peterhead Prison in an attempt to persuade him to grant me a visit. It was a straightforward request, open and honest, advising him that I was writing a book covering events from 1989 to the present. In truth, I never expected a reply, but I was still disappointed as each week passed without a prison-stamped envelope falling through my letterbox.

I wasn't after a confession; nor was I interested in giving him a platform from which to profess his innocence or point accusatory fingers at the police. All that I wanted was to satisfy my curiosity about the man I had heard and read so much about.

Some of the people I had spoken to who have met Ian Beggs after he was convicted of the murder of Barry Wallace had described him as formidable – strong, confident and somewhat intimidating, both intellectually and in the way he presented himself physically. Others who I have had the opportunity to interview who knew Beggs from when he was a schoolboy, and later as a young man obsessed with politics, remember a rather meek, non-confrontational, slightly awkward figure.

In prison, of course, where survival of the fittest, if not the most popular, is still very much the credo, Ian Beggs would have had to reinvent himself. And, from his many legal skirmishes with the courts and the prison authorities over the last ten years, on his own behalf and that of many of his fellow inmates, it is apparent that this is exactly what he has done.

Within weeks of beginning his life term, while still in Saughton Prison, Beggs was refusing food and demanding to be moved to an area of the jail inhabited by inmates who were drug free. Not surprisingly, this was to mark the beginning of a catalogue of episodes of disruptive behaviour by Ian Beggs, aimed at challenging whoever and whatever represented his continuing incarceration. He may have lost control of his life, locked up in a cell the majority of the day, being told when and where he could go, but he must have gained some satisfaction from becoming a permanent headache for the authorities. If he had known that he was soon to be moved to Peterhead Prison, though, he may have thought twice about rocking the boat at Saughton.

The journey to Peterhead from Edinburgh is fairly lengthy, the town lying far up on the east coast in Aberdeenshire. For any of his relatives choosing to visit him there, it would involve either a ferry journey followed by a drive right across the breadth of Scotland, or alternatively a flight into Aberdeen itself and thereafter a hire car or taxi. Either way, it would be a laborious trek and rather expensive for just a single visit. The little flat at Kilmarnock was still available for a stop-over, of course, but I am not sure whether anyone would have wanted to spend much time there, knowing what had happened in the spare bedroom. With this in mind, and realising that he was being categorised as a sex offender within the prison system, Beggs could not have been best pleased.

Apart from his appeal against conviction, one of the more lengthy petitions which Beggs had lodged with the courts was consideration that he be transferred from Peterhead to Edinburgh, so that he would have more direct accessibility to his legal team. There were other reasons for wanting a transfer, of course, besides the practical ones as previously stated, but he knew that they alone would not secure a move. The original decision to send Beggs to Peterhead was made by the Scottish Prison Service, and based on the fact that he was considered a long-term sex offender; as such, he would be best located in that jail, which already housed several similar type inmates.

According to Beggs' legal team, such was the complexity of his appeal, requiring numerous consultations and frequent contact with counsel, that they believed that progress was being hindered by the fact that the prison was not within easy reach of Edinburgh and, as a result, they were often ill-prepared for short-notice hearings.

It didn't help matters, though, when throughout the appeal process Beggs would change his legal team on a whim, and continued to demand major input into how matters were being handled. He was, however, granted a short transfer to Edinburgh on 4 May 2004, but was returned just four weeks later on 4 June. It was considered extremely unlikely that his petition would have been disposed of within that period, but there was no extension of the term. In ruling, the Lord Ordinary, presiding over a further petition to grant an interim declarator in the matter, stated that he did not believe that the petitioner (Beggs) was significantly hindered in any way from communicating with his legal team by way of post, telephone or even face to face. He referred to the 33 visits from legal representatives which had already taken place at Peterhead, as well as the 540 telephone calls and the 111 legal privileged letters he had received to date. The eventual ruling by Lord Carloway in March 2005 upheld every aspect of the Lord Ordinary's previous decision, and Beggs remained in Peterhead.

Some of the more bizarre stories making headlines years after Beggs' conviction were those which reported his antics while in jail. One story suggested that he was taking woodworking lessons in the prison, learning to use a saw, among other tools, on a nine-month course, for which he would have had to have passed an interview. Considering his dismemberment of Barry Wallace, the article was not necessarily in the best taste. Nor was another report which said that Beggs was temporarily employed in the jail as the barber, with other inmates apparently putting their lives in peril by trusting the 'gay ripper' with scissors and such like. The stories may have had some truth, of course, but were hardly headline news. What was apparent to newspaper editors, though, was the fact that the public still had an appetite for all sorts of information about the 'monster', and continued to do so long after the trial had ended.

Aside from the titillation, Beggs was making real news. From being a suspected serial killer, he was now earning his reputation as a serial litigant, the instigator of one legal challenge after another on behalf of himself and other inmates, on issues which in few cases were sufficiently well founded. The greater implications of such actions were, of course, the strain on the taxpayer, as Beggs and others were being granted legal aid to take the cases to court. What he had done as a free man on the outside, challenging the State and the authorities, he was continuing to do on the inside. This was something which I suspect was giving him some purpose and stimulation, as well as a modicum of respect from his fellow inmates.

Besides winning the right to gain access to a computer with which to work on his own appeal, Beggs had taken it upon himself to act on behalf of his fellow inmates in a challenge to the archaic practice of 'slopping out'. In prisons dating back to the 1800s, such as Peterhead, where there were no sanitary facilities included in cells, prisoners were still required to use a small plastic pot if caught short during the night. When let out the following morning, they were then required to empty their buckets in a routine dubbed 'slopping out'. According to the press, several of his fellow inmates had won compensation for such inhumane treatment as a result of his taking the matter to court, with as much as £2,000 being paid to one or more individuals, of which Beggs reportedly took a 15 per cent cut for his expertise.

Prison rules stated that no inmate was permitted to receive payment for services provided inside the jail, but it didn't seem to deter Beggs. On agreeing to provide the necessary paperwork with which to lodge an action on an individual's behalf, Beggs would insist his cut was paid by postal order after the monies awarded had been paid into the applicant's bank account. There was, of course, no real way of enforcing payment, and, according to insiders in the jail, he had few allies to whom he could turn if someone decided simply to ignore his protestations. But because of his legal expertise, most of which derived from his many brushes with the establishment and from the lectures he was taking in law as part of a degree he had applied for, there was a 'grudging' respect.

The single most significant action he undertook was the bid to win compensation for inmates at Peterhead who had been denied the right to vote, basing his argument on the fact that they had been denied their basic human rights. Potentially, this was an enormous case, which if won would mean that each and every inmate in all the jails in Scotland, not just Peterhead, could be eligible for a substantial payout.

At first, Beggs and a few others had made applications to the local Electoral Registration Officer to be able to vote, and were subsequently denied. They then took their case to court, but it was thrown out, only to be granted an appeal to a future court date at which they could argue their point.

That date came in October 2008, and a full-scale security operation had to be put in place as Beggs and seven other inmates were transported to Aberdeen Sheriff Court at which they were each given an opportunity to put forward their submissions to Sheriff Colin Harris. Another six inmates' cases were heard, although they did not appear in person. Each appellant represented themselves on the day, some obviously more eloquently than others. For some of the eight who had been transported the 30 miles from the jail in two separate groups, one in the morning and the other in the afternoon, it was a jolly, of course; a day away from the drudgery of prison life, and a chance to have a voice in open court.

For Ian Beggs, however, it was a stage, where he took full advantage of his opportunity and filled an hour of the court's time with his polished argument. Dressed in a blue blazer, white shirt and black trousers, Beggs was said to have carried with him a bundle of legal reference books. In his submission, Beggs pointed out that he recognised the problem as a purely practical one, where it was extremely difficult logistically to get each and every prisoner to a ballot box, and not, as some would imagine, a 'punitive' measure based on the inmate's criminal record and incarceration.

Neither Beggs nor Sheriff Harris would have been under any illusions that the case would be decided at a local domestic court level, but that was the route that had to be taken before it could be considered within the European Court of Human Rights. The Sheriff even referred to the hearing as a mere 'stepping stone'.

Stepping stone or not, with the extra security, the transport and feeding arrangements and the full day set aside for the hearings, the little escapade at Aberdeen Sheriff Court had cost taxpayers somewhere in the region of £10,000. But working on the basis that each of the 7,000 inmates in the Scottish prison system would receive around £1,000 in compensation should they actually win their case, that £10,000 pounds would be a mere fraction of the potential eventual payout.

I doubt anyone would dispute that, regardless of circumstances, our basic human rights are sacrosanct and, in that respect, we should have no issue with a legitimate challenge such as this may have been. But what causes much anger is the fact that the majority of these actions, many of which are spurious, are funded by the ordinary man in the street. Furthermore, the victims left behind by Beggs and his fellow offenders will indirectly, through taxation, be assisting in seeing these matters brought before an already overloaded legal system. This continual defiance displayed by Beggs, the product of which I believe serves only to provide gratification for him, will continue to keep his name in the newspapers. In some way, that will be a positive lest some of us forget why he is in prison in the first place, and need reminding of his heinous crimes.

Equally damning are the names he has been linked to through offering his 'legal' services within one prison establishment or another. In 2008, the *Daily Record* reported that the so-called 'Da Vinci Code' rapist, Robert Greens, had used Beggs' services, as had paedophile John Bermingham. Later in 2009, while Beggs was in Saughton Prison awaiting the start of his appeal hearing in Edinburgh the following month, inmate Kevin Fyffe, a convicted rapist and serial offender who was dubbed 'The Thing', had approached him, and Beggs had agreed to coach him on an appeal against a decision made by the courts to revoke his licence, even though the matters he had been reported for on his initial release from jail had been dropped.

I would be very surprised if someone as intelligent as Ian Beggs does not recognise the negative impact these associations may have on any future plans he has for release, considering the recent loss of his appeal. Perhaps he should consider trying to keep a lower profile, gradually fading away in people's memory, without constantly reminding them of his existence by courting the press as he does.

Interestingly enough, one of his fellow inmates, who is arguably a more sinister figure, but whose name seldom appears anywhere lest it be in connection with his original crimes, is that of serial killer Peter Tobin, the man convicted of the murders of Angelika Kluk, Vicky Hamilton and Dinah McNicol. Tobin, whose reign of terror took place over a 15-year period from 1991 to 2006, is rumoured to have bragged in jail about dozens more murders for which he was responsible. He, too, had been represented during his trial for murdering Kluk and Hamilton by Donald Findlay QC, a fact which may have given Beggs and Tobin something to discuss on the long winter evenings during association time in the prison.

There will, of course, be no release for Tobin, whose life sentence for Dinah McNicol's murder was stipulated as natural life. As a result, one might reasonably expect him to confess to whatever unsolved crimes he may be responsible for, and give closure to the families of victims still waiting for answers. But like Ian Beggs and other killers, in many ways, having had his opportunity to commit crimes taken from him by his incarceration, Tobin may need to retain control of something within his life. In his case, that control and empowerment may come from the retention of information; the knowledge of all that he has done outweighing his convictions. It is possible that Ian Beggs is in the same position to reveal the extent of his crimes, but as he still has an opportunity to be released sometime in the future, it is unlikely that he would consciously and so blatantly jeopardise that possibility by admitting his guilt.

I was never under any illusions that either William or Winifred Beggs would ever agree to talk to me about their son, and tell how coping with the everyday realities of the consequences of his crimes had affected them. Other than the issues they took with their arrest and detention by the Strathclyde Police, they have said little to the press over the last ten years or so, and nothing I would say would be likely to change their minds. I did, however, make an approach to Ian Beggs' uncle, Fred Crowe, the former Ulster Unionist

Lord Mayor of Craigavon, and the man who possibly shaped his nephew's interest in politics. Of all the family, he had been the most vocal in dismissing the charges made against Ian Beggs, and I wanted to see if his opinion had changed since the loss of the appeal.

It was to be a brief telephone conversation, and one which I can only describe as being rather surreal. After a short introduction, Mr Crowe, who I had been told was slightly under the weather and staying with a relative in England, began by telling me that in his opinion I was rather unwise to be considering printing anything about Ian Beggs. According to him, the appeal against sentence and conviction was still ongoing and that I would best consider my position and wait until matters had been concluded. He was at pains to remind me of the 'prejudicial' reporting which he said had been a bone of contention during the original trial, and how anything I would write would be considered the same.

I had to point out to Mr Crowe that, as far as I was aware, Ian Beggs had lost his appeal in March this year and, even more recently, his bid to launch a further appeal through the UK's Supreme Court had been denied by the three judges on the panel, Lord Eassie, Lady Paton and Lord Bannatyne. In respect of material gathered for the book, I advised him that anything I had written to date about Ian Beggs was already in the public domain as such, and that I was relying on the facts as most people would see them to tell the story. But my comments were falling on deaf ears.

Referring to the murder of Barry Oldham back in 1987, and the original trial and conviction which was overturned on appeal just two years later, Fred Crowe stated that it had been done so not on a technicality, but on the basis of Ian Beggs' outright innocence. In his words, it was the 'facts' of the case which were wrong and which cleared Ian of that charge. In his next breath, when I could hear someone in the background clearly telling him not to say anything further, Mr Crowe again warned me about printing anything which I could regret, and that he was surprised that I had nothing better to do with my time than to write a story about his nephew.

The most alarming part of the conversation, as far as I was concerned, was not the veiled threats of litigation, for I am in no doubt that is what they were, but the sheer naïvety of the man. I could possibly have misinterpreted naïvety for bare-faced front, of course, but the arguments and rhetoric were not that of an intelligent individual. What Mr Crowe has simply ignored in his oversimplistic analysis of events is the overwhelming, real and indisputable evidence which supports the fact that William Ian Frederick Beggs is a cold-blooded killer who has ruined many lives along his path of destruction. There is no conspiracy against him.

When I first met Brian McQuillan in London, I was genuinely struck by his quiet, unassuming nature, even though I knew he had shown a tremendous amount of courage when faced with a man who intended to take his life. There are no hidden agendas with Brian – what you see is what you get. If you are lucky enough to count him among one of your friends, then you will not have far to look for honesty, compassion and loyalty.

In a sense, those attributes are the exact opposing qualities to those of Ian Beggs, and may have acted as the key to halting his trail of murder when it did. Without Brian McQuillan surviving the attack at Doon Place, and the local police becoming reacquainted with Beggs' offending history, then who knows how many more people may have suffered injury or death in the little spare bedroom. After Beggs was investigated for attacking Brian McQuillan in 1991, his name was put to the top of their list as a potentially violent offender with a history of cutting or slashing men living within their area. He was well and truly on the radar as far as police were concerned, and that is why they beat a path to his door when Barry Wallace was murdered.

One could never describe Ian Beggs as brave or courageous, for his crimes are opportunistic and cowardly. Nor could you ever rely on him for compassion or loyalty, for he is self-centred and heartless. As far as honesty is concerned, Beggs has never been able to tell the truth about anything, whether it be for something quite simple as on his application for the post of housing officer at Kilmarnock and Loudoun Council, or about something more complex like the truth surrounding his sexual orientation. His whole life appears to have been constructed around one lie or another and, in terms of any future review board considering his release after minimum term, attention must be drawn to that dishonesty.

For some people serving long terms in prison, reform is possible, particularly those who have committed their crimes in the early, more formative years of their lives. One moment of madness perhaps, a troubled childhood promoting anger and frustration and culminating in a mindless act.

Living in Northern Ireland after the Good Friday Agreement, many of us will have had to accept that, as part of the terms of that agreement, several inmates serving prison sentences for dreadful acts of murder committed over the time of the Troubles have been freed from jail long before their sentences would have been complete. Of course, those prison releases are unique in the sense that they were considered a necessary part of placing the past behind us and looking towards a future free from violence. For one reason or another, we can learn to accept that, in some cases, indefinite incarceration is either unsustainable or counter-productive.

Should I be around long enough to see Ian Beggs released back into the community at whatever age, then I fear the system will have failed. The 'gay ripper', or 'the beast' as he was referred to in many newspaper reports, is a reasonable description for someone who will always represent a danger to the public, and must be kept caged. I fear for any panel charged with making that decision if it arises, but trust they remember, before anything else, that their first considerations are for the mothers, fathers, sons, daughters, brothers and sisters all around these islands and further, who could one day be looking towards them and asking why they opened the cell door and let this man back into society to cause pain and heartbreak once again.